DISCARD

The Music Stopped and your Monkey's On Fire

David Plumb

Wings Press
Houston

© 1979 Wings Press
Printed in the USA

ISBN 0-930324-10-2 (Hardback)
ISBN 0-930324-11-0 (Paperback)
Library of Congress 78-73262

Wings Press
P.O. Box 25296
Houston, Texas 77005
713-668-7953

for Julia

COME TO THE FUN HOUSE...FIFTY-THREE CENTS...Come to the Fun House...the spirit is a Fraud my friend..COME TO THE FUN HOUSE...SIT by the lowwuuuung guhreeen poooowell...a drum your fingers on the edge...WATCH the men WATCH the naked men hold each other in UNison... LOOK at the BEEEEEOOOOOTIFUL BODIES friend...The SPIRIT is a FRAUD FIFTY-THREE CENTS...you KNOW it doesn't exist if it did exist it wouldn't try and TRICK you friend... SPIRITS don't bleed my friend..they don't SUCK you friend... FIFTY-THREE CENTS COME TO THE FUN HOUSE...LOOK at your friend's COCK friend...who's your FRIEND friend?.. this is an illusion an illusion this is...FIFTY-THREE CENTS...I wouldn't try and TRICK you friend...WOULD IT try and trick you friend?...INTROspection...just LOOK at my NICE BUULAACK HAT friend.. just LOOK at my NICE BUULAACK HAT...come right in..the price is concrete blood FIFTY-THREE CENTS WORTH OF CONCRETE BLOOD...we ALL need BLOOD friend...Step right up step right up...for that price you can buy a shallow will EVERYbody wants a shallow will EVERYbody...Come IN and see her in the bedroom friend see her in the FRIEND'S bedroom friend FIFTY-three cents.. money comes so hard what IS it you WANT friend?..I can't bark all day don't let the BIG BAD WOLF lookya in the EYE friend..if he does ya might get a HARD on for TWENTY-FIVE CENTS EXTRA YOU can have ID SALAD .. can YOU CHOOSE your own source of insatiability friend?..now I ASK you little friend?...WHERE did you GET those SHORT PANTS?..Nobody wears short pants anymore..MAYBE you're OLDer just OLDer than you LOOK...you'll have to PARDon my BUULAAACK HAT FIFTY-THREE CENTS COME to the Fun House would'ja like a little PREview friend?..

SEE IT BELIEVE IT . . there she IZZZZZ . . IZZZN'T she BEEEOOOOOTIFUL friend? . . you look unHAPPY friend for TWENTY-FIVE CENTS EXTRA YOU CAN WATCH HER FUCK A PYGMIE friend . . NOWWWWWW you are being GENNNNERRALLY INTerested friend I can SEE that . . well WATCHYA goin ta DOOOOO I can't talk forever? . . and the WOLF may be LIFE friend ever thinka THAT but for FIFTY-THREE CENTS you TOO can find out who the WEEEEZzulls are . . WHERE is the VEIN friend? . . for TWENTY-FIVE CENTS EXTRA you can find the vein and FIFTY-THREE CENTS COME TO the Fun House and not SEEEE her again and WHAT would her MOTHER say and WHAT would her FATHER say and WHAT would YOUUUU like to say about my NICE . . BULLAACK . . HATlittle friend? . . what do you THINK of my FIIIINE BUULAAACK HAT little friend? . . .SEE THE umBRELLA duel . . SEE the AFRIcan Dance costumes FIFTY-THREE CENTS you can't kill umBRELLA but you can WATCH . . look at the looowwuuung guuhreen poooowell WHISper from the BALcony only FIFTY-THREE CENTS . . LOOK through the TRANS. . .parent BUUreasts. . .LOOK!

TABLE OF CONTENTS

1. Fifty-Three Cents 4

2. Little Round Harmonica 11

3. Destroyer Tender 25

4. Camping Out 29

5. She Was Always Sunday 35

6. Well Annyyyywaaaayyy 41

7. Ambulance 45

8. Alan Ladd Meets the Emigrant
   From Oakland 63

9. Sherlock Goes to the Vet 67

10. Southern Comfort 73

11. Embarcadero Center 75

THE MUSIC STOPPED AND YOUR MONKEY'S ON FIRE

fiction by

DAVID PLUMB

The Little Round Harmonica

-Mom, oh Mom, Mom. The door bounced against the wall and Caroline's books spilled on the floor. She ran into her mother's waist crying. -They said I wasn't sexy and that I'm ugly and they chased me home. Mommy I feel awful! I'm uuuuggggllyyy and it feels awwwwfullll!

-Who said? Davies stuck his chin out and stalked to the window. -Who?

-Everybody.

-Where are they? There was nobody in sight. Jake waved from the gas station and Davies waved back. -Well, I think you're. . .I mean, you're not ugly.

-No you're not honey. What made them, no listen it's ok. . . Why did they say that?

-Becuz, becuz I wouldn't. . . .She broke into tears again. -They wanted me to go over to Hester's house and. . . . Oh Mommy I'm uuuggglly!

-Come on now, who wanted you to do what?

Heather. . .Heather. . .and her friends. They well, you know, Heather's mother works Tuesdays and we like to go over there and play and well, they were gonna have the boys over and play, well, and I didn't like it to. . . .

-Oh?!

-Oh, Mommy I'm sorry, I'm just soooo ugly and I'm not even sexxxxy! She buried her face in Nadene's sweater.

-You're NOT ugly, Brad said. -In fact we think you're beautiful, don't we Mommy?

-Of course we do.

-But they said. . .
-Forget what they said. Never mind them. Come on over here honey. Brad sat her on the couch next to him.
-Now I knew this ole gal in San Francisco who used to. . . . Why Caroline, she was the ugliest ole thing you ever saw, all wrinkles and warts. And she used to dance in the streets in her socks. She had long old socks, red ones that hung way over her toes like big floppy worms' tails. Why she was so ugly, you wouldn't think anybody wanted her and tough. . .Lemmie tell ya. Somebody loved her.
-Somebody did?
-And she lived under the street.
-How did she live under the street and find somebody?
-Didn't find him under the street. Found him in the Palm Garden. That's a big restaurant up on Market Street with pictures of flags and knights and shields and they have a big steam table and lots of brown tables and you can get two rainbow trout with green sauce for two seventy-five, at least you could, but that's where she met him. And there's a long bar and oh, outside they have a seafood bar with clams and oysters and. . . .
-Yuk.
-Anyway, Harriet, that was her name. Harriet. Harriet didn't always have enough money to buy a meal, so sometimes she'd just sit over in a corner and wait for somebody to leave and eat what was left.
-Oh she did not. That's awful.
-Yes she did. And on this rainy day, it was a Sunday and she was sitting in the corner watching. . . .Way down at the other end of the table, there was a little guy with crutches and only one arm eating corn beef. Most of his

hair was gone and he had a face like a sparrow.

-Like Quentin's arm?

-Cut off just below the elbow. Anyway, all of a sudden one of the men who worked there came over and started yelling at the guy saying, You stole my wrenches and, We're gonna get the cops and the guy's gotta mouthful of potatoes and he looks up and tries to tell the guy he doesn't have any wrenches, but the guy grabs his shirtsleeve, the one with the arm missing and shakes it. And what do you think happened?

-The guy hit him with the other arm.

-Nope. A whole bunch of wrenches fell out of the sleeve onto the table. And brother, the first thing ya know the other guy was goin for the cops and the poor old guy was tryin to get his crutches working, had a piece of corned beef hangin right outta his mouth makin for the back door and ole Harriet, she just sidles down the chairs as slick as can be and slides the plate across and begins eatin like nothin ever happened.

-And right next to her is this other skinny guy lookin like he might blow away and she suddenly gets worried cause he's got a short-sleeved shirt on like the cooks, only he's eatin too. She gets to watchin his pointed elbows shovelling up the pot roast and spaghetti and he isn't paying any attention to her at all, so she eats a little faster. Finally, he finishes and looks over at her. She's sittin on his right, and he bends over to take a closer look and sees the big fat mole on the left side of her chin has a hair on it and she stops for a second.

-What was you looking at?

-I was lookin at you.

-Zat all ya gotta do is stare at people while they eat?
-I work over at Breen's on Third.
-So?
-I thought I saw you walkin up the alley one day.
-Might've. What of it? Can't a person walk up an alley without somebody talkin? She wiped the plate with the roll and stuffed it in her mouth.
-The plate?
-Caroline.
-And he tells her she's got pretty hair and she does have pretty hair. Had it tied back in a bun. Real gray and soft and held up by a brown hair comb.

Turned out, he'd been in the hospital with a heart attack, lost a whole buncha weight and was working at the restaurant, but ate at the Palm Garden so he wouldn't be stuck with the same food. She finally admitted she lived close by and well, for some reason, and pretty soon it got to be a habit, he was watchin for her long green skirt and the big long brown scarf she always wore around her neck and the long blue coat that never buttoned and flapped at the back of her calves. She was different when she was on the street alone. Her feet bounced off the sidewalk and she raised her arms to feel the wind and the way she walked, it was like a dance, you could never think of her as being ugly, why nobody could touch that kind of beauty, they couldn't hurt her at all and Ken the Cook sure liked that. Even got jealous when a truckdriver honked and she waved. And she was sixty-one years old.

-That's old.
-No it isn't. And one day about three weeks later, Ken saw her headin down towards Howard, that's two blocks south of Market and parallel. They'd cleared away some of the

buildings and there were cyclone fences around the lots and he watched her make a turn and disappear to the right offa Third. So he gets curious and follows her and when he gets to where she turned he sees a path along the side of the fence that leads to an opening a few hundred feet back, never know it was there just lookin from the street, and down there in what used to be the cellar of some old building, was Harriet. She's walking across the lot towards a bunch of caves under the street and when she gets there she takes off her coat and hangs it up on an old beam sticking outta the concrete overhead. Then she sat down on some old broken sidewalk and began taking her hair down. She sat there in the sun and combed that long gray hair, why it came right down to her waist and shined in the light like long silky spiderwebs and old Ken got to thinkin about his heart condition and how he needed a shave and how his ear itched and how he wanted to put on weight so he could get back up to a hundred and sixty and how he hadda watch the salt.

-The next day when she came dancing down the street, he was waiting for her, all shaved and combed, had a green wool sweater on and shined shoes, why she came dancin by him and he just began dancin right along side a her. At first she didn't notice, then in a corner of her eye she saw this smile smilin at her and she made a little turn and a hummph and stopped dancin. Walked right off like she was mindin her business and he came right alongside and began talkin a blue streak about her hair and how beautiful it was and would she like to go to a movie and she was thinkin she hadn't been to a movie in a long time, didn't think much of movies cause they never told the truth no how. But it was a nice thought anyway, she'd have to say no, but he wasn't having any of that, just kept tellin her how pretty she was and she kept sayin it was all bull and by the time they got to Mission and Third, she remembered she didn't want anybody to know where she lived, least nobody she didn't know. Why she left her family fifteen years ago, husband died and kids didn't want her around, didn't want to work for anyone anymore anyhow, not gonna let the first guy that comes along, but he looked alright she thought giving him the once over with those sharp brown eyes that Ken thought looked almost black and scared him a little.

-Didn't he talk her into it?! Even talked her into a meal afterwards, but she wouldn't let him walk her home. Even bought some popcorn in the movies. . . .

-But he already knew where she lived. And what about the salt? How come he was worried about salt?

-Cause heart patients have to watch how much salt they take. And sure he knew where she lived, but didn't you ever know somethin and figure it might be better to let the other person tell you so you wouldn't spoil anything?

-Well sometimes.

-And soooo. . .It wasn't very long before they were seein each other kinda regular, but not too regular, cause Harriet wasn't used to havin people around very long, although she had to admit to herself he was growin on her.

-Along about this time, she heard they were gettin ready to clean out the place she lived in to rebuild and she began to worry about where she was gonna move to. Word was they'd start work in about three weeks, two days after her sixty-second birthday and she told Ken about it. He didn't seem surprised that she lived under the street, but he did look worried. Course he knew where she lived. Don't you be worryin

16

about this ole thing, she told him. Why I've hadda move more times, this ain't gonna be nothin different, but two days after my birthday gits me right here. And she slapped her butt.

Got to thinkin maybe *he* wasn't feelin too good and started stoppin by Breen's and waitin for him after work. Didn't come in at first, just hung around by the side entrance once or twice until she was sure he wanted her around. Ken's boss said something to him about it, but didn't make an issue. Thing was, as much as Harriet loved it under the street, she was gettin more anxious every time she left it. Thinkin maybe she'd come home some night and it wouldn't be there anymore, so she'd hang around the streets a little longer and look in the store windows a little later and tell Ken she was worried about his health, while Ken's doctor had told him he'd be alright. Do anything he wanted as long as he watched the salt.

-On her birthday, he forgot about salt and got off work early. They went up to Chinatown to a place called the Jackson Cafe and he bought her Jackson Steamed Clams and Jackson Chow Mein and Ginger Oysters with Green Onions over Rice and nobody said anything about her not having any shoes on. She worried they might throw her out, although she confessed she'd been thrown out of worse places. Ken said ta hell they will and why they just stuffed themselves and drank tea lookin at each other like a coupla school kids.

-I'm a school kid.
-That's what I'm gettin at.
-But you said I'm not ugly.
-That's right, you're not.
-Well how come?
-You'll see. And afterwards, they went for a walk up to Coit Tower and looked at the Bay, wasn't even any fog, and then

they went down around the Embarcadero where all the ships used to come in before they started going to Oakland, where it's long and gray and the rotting pilings and old restaurants and piers lurk beside the water that slaps slaps away in the night and sometimes shines in the light of the city, or passing cars or the moon and they heard cars passing way off somewhere. Once in awhile one passed them as if they didn't exist and it made them smile to think they were in a place where the railroad tracks crossed and the warehouses were closed and old boxcars sat along the other side of the street so wide you almost couldn't tell where the other side was, why that street goes all the way around the North end of the City and Harriet said she heard they were gonna tear *it* down too and put God knows what all there. They both agreed it would be a sad thing because there was gettin to be no place for some people to go, then they stopped for a couple of minutes to watch the cars way off up in front of them going back and forth across the Bay Bridge, the cars leaving on the lower tier and coming on the top one and they got to talkin about how it made em feel little again, lookin up at all those cars with their lights on goin some place and how good it felt to dream like that and at the same time, how wonderful it was to be where they were, just walkin along a lonely street when everbody's gone home and you can hear yourself breathe if you listen, and the ships in the fog when there was fog, blowin their horns like some old school teacher with a round harmonica givin you the key to the song so you can begin, but you've already begun, so you listen to the next time because there's always fog and you hope there'll always be foghorns and Ken said it was sometimes nice to sit on the edge of the Bay and watch the ships at night and try to figure out how long they are, or

whether they're fishing boats, or maybe a tug pushing a barge, then there'd be an amber light and it's always inland when you see an amber light and he slipped his hand into hers as they walked slowly South along the wide circling street that comes to an end by the drawbridge on Third Street where all the trains live.
  -At the end of the long low building with the sign over the double doors that says ENGINE-9, SFFD, FIRE BOAT-1, there's a hydrant. Ken said the chain coming from the front plug looked like a watchchain stuck under a man's hat and Harriet said the metal around the streetlight next to it looked like a queen's crown as she looked over her shoulder at the clock on the Ferry Building easing into nine minutes of eleven far behind them. They both decided that the moon reflecting on the crossbeams under the bridge painted a picture that didn't seem real from where they stood. It was something you couldn't take your eyes off and didn't know why. Began to get chilly then, so they walked a little faster. Now Harriet was sticking her finger in the telephone coin returns. -Nothing she said out loud. -Nothing. You know what I'd like to do?
  -No I don't.
  -See that sign up there?
  -Where?
  -Right over our heads.
  -The ENTRANCE sign.
  -The first N is missing.
  -So?
  -So I've always wanted to stick my finger in the empty N, but I'm not tall enough. Thought about climbing up. Could probably reach it. Never got around to it.
  -I can't reach it either. Buuuuut. . .

-No you don't, not with that heart.

-Ain't nothing. And just like that, he picked her up and held her high enough so she could put that finger in the N of the ENTRANCE sign.

Well lemmie tell ya, that just about made her night. She couldn't get over it. Didn't bother with another phone booth. They crossed the Embarcadero...

-What's an Embarcero?

-It's the name of the street along the waterfront. And on the other side where the railroad tracks are, Harriet pointed out the fact that there are five tracks on the North side of Townsend and ten on the South side, four coming off the first one and two a them goin on down the Embarcadero and two swinging off to the right towards second. Actually five if ya wanna count the one in the middle that goes right across the block. Two, three and four stay the same except for a cross from three to four and five has three branchin off it with a cross over at the end of First Street going over to four in the middle, makes eight goin around between the buildings towards Second Street, but Four goes back ta three at Second, but ya can't see em very well in the dark unless ya walk along em.

-Ken was eyein the sign on the left side a Townsend that said GLOBE WALLY'S inc, FORK LIFT SERVICE. Up on Second, just offa Townsend they stopped to peek into the pumphouse. All the brass was polished and the pipes were shining and there was a high ceiling with big clean wide floors below the balcony. Up to the right someone had hung a female mannequin. Harriet thought she'd like to go down there and dance and Ken said why don'cha and seein nobody seemed to be around, she went down the iron stops to her left and went out on that floor. Right in the center, she reached back and pulled the comb out of her hair and shook her head and that hair fell so smooth around her shoulders Ken got a chill. Then she went up on her toes and began to dance her own special ballet across the smooth floor and around the gleaming brass plugs and red painted pumps and pipes. . .

-Brad, you said the pipes were all brass.

-Some of em were and her heels were barely touching the floor and those ole socks bobbing out to the side of her feet, her scarf trailing when she didn't lift her arms as she turned to look up at him smiling in an embarassed little way because there wasn't any music, but the more he thought about it, the more he realized there was music getting louder and louder, then softer and softer and finally slipping away as she dipped beneath him and came up the stairs.

-There was really music. From where?

Davies tapped his head. -There, everybody's got it. So they left the pumphouse and Harriet didn't even bother to put up her hair. The walk up Second was quieter than it had ever been for her.

At first she didn't want to do it, but she did it. She went up to his hotel room that had a single bed and a dresser and a sink and a little table by the window with a candle on it, a small bottle of wine and some daisies in a water glass and they lit the candle and drank the wine from the bottle because there was only one other glass. Sitting there on the side of the bed, they could watch the man leaning on the parked cars across the street talking back and forth in Italian over the dwindling traffic.

-Happy Birthday.

-Yes, Happy Birthday.

-He blew out the candle and they got undressed and stood looking at each other in the light from the street.

-God damn, he said.
-God damn, she said.
-Why'd they say that? Caroline flopped back on the couch.
-Cause they liked what they saw.
-What did they see?
-They saw each other.
-But you said she was ugly?
-Lemmie tell ya later. Ken didn't see her the next day and figured she was lookin for a new place. Saw her that evening, but she was way up the block and walking real fast. He wondered if he'd done something wrong. Later that night he drank more beer than he should have at the Palm Garden.
-The next morning he got up early and shaved, got a cuppa coffee and went down to the building site. He could hear the bulldozer moving around and he began running. When he got to the fence, it was parked by the section they'd pulled back next to the path. It was clearing up and the light rain from the night before made everything look bright and washed. Even the bulldozer. Down in the lot Harriet was watching that bulldozer as she pulled the comb out of her hair and tucked it in her pocket. She didn't see Ken behind the fence. She began to dance. Very slowly and deliberately, all around the lot, touching everything she passed with a light hand or finger and on between the broken stone and rubble like they were nothing to worry about anyway. By the time Ken got over to the bulldozer, the man was revving it up.
-Lookit that fool woman. The bulldozer began to move.
-I'm lookin, Ken said following slowly. -I'm lookin.
-Halfway down the bulldozer stopped because Harriet had suddenly made a run right towards him. She stopped dead about ten feet away, put her hands on her hips and stared at the

window she couldn't see through because of the light's reflection on the glass. Her feet were planted tight on the ground and her socks looked defiant.

-I'll get your bag. Ken started for the blanket tied at the corners. She put her left hand on his arm without taking her eyes off the bulldozer. -Keep your hands off it. I carry my own. Ken stared at the bulldozer. It idled outrageously.

Finally Harriet walked over and got her blanket, threw it over her right shoulder and came back to Ken's side. Both of them waited for another long minute before stepping out of its way.
-So?
-That's the end.
-That's the end? Why?
-Cause that's the end.
-Well, what happened?
-They left together.
-But I mean, didn't they get married?
-I dunno.

Destroyer Tender

Radio blaring, carnival painted jeepneys running from one war to another took almost everybody someplace. One of them nearly clipped Brad Davies, then careened wildly into thick traffic. An eighth of a mile behind him, the yellow river ran quietly among the reeds around the lower end of town and under the concrete bridge where the sailors came from base to town and back. There, the white-slacked san pan girls begged and little brothers dove for centavos, pennies, quarters, anything now and then, while the Shore Patrol waited townside with local police, who'd rather throw a street whore into the water (put em out of commission, cheaper than arrest), inching past more san pans tied to shore, shacks roofed to impossible poverty clinging to the edges and the face of a pig that appeared, then disappeared after seeming to stand dumbly forever watching the river flow out to who knows where the sea started. No matter how far into the belly of town he walked, Davies couldn't shake the smell of the river.

Backtown hammocks swung gently, or not at all in dimlit rooms with wall-stricken crucifixes, and mothers of mothers' daughters turning tricks, held the Again Children breathing softly just before the sky dropped streaks of pink. The sun pulled darkness down the surrounding hills and hawkers' charcoal began to glow in the dusty sweat-necked horn honking country western sergeant pepper sock it to me baby night, screaming bar to bar, hotel to hotel, restaurant to restaurant and pork onion monkey pancit rice soy pepper stale beer and urine lingered amidst an extravaganza of gigantic hanging monkeypod scissors knives forks, monkeypod dolls animals plates bowls salad bowls statues and nutcracker dolls with metal crotches, keychains, under the table butterfly knives, beads, snoopy rings, dice, dice cups, here and there a sanimanok, postcards of fishermen, Baguio and Manila. If-You-Want-It-Ask City of Olongopo, slowly criss-crossed shadows beneath neon blinking in any crevice capable of holding a sign and white hats bobbed up everywhere, earrings jingled, kids stole and sold anything, shining capped teeth flashed with rustled pesos, the dull thunk of green San Miguel in front of him and the half-final change, laid on the table, as he leaned back in the chair to help the night go mad.

    Some of the chicks had pet baby chicks and some of the guys had chicks with baby chicks and some of the guys had onetwothree baby chicks they bought on the street and some of the guys didn't want chicks, they wanted to drink, or had fed their baby chicks to the alligator in front of Pauline's (the best bar in Olongopo some said) and some of the guys put pretty yellow baby chicks in their vest pockets that weren't supposed to have anything in them, not even I.D. cards, so all they had to do was inhale to keep those chicks in line and up front, a young Filipino stepped on stage, pulled the brushes from his green spangled drums and drew them easily over the snare. The sound system barely picked them up. At the left corner of the stage, the other musicians hunched over cigarettes with pupils high in the whites of their eyes, blowing easy smoke around the cool chicks leaning, or always about to lean on their shoulders.

    Davies ordered another beer and by the time it came, tables all around were full of chicks in laps and baby chicks pecking ashtrays beer bottles, cellophane, ashes, cocked back white hats, more chicks, she had long black hair coming almost to her thighs and some of it got hung up underneath when she sat on his lap and threw her arms around him. -You like Ocean Eleven, no? Shanghai Club, Zanzibar, maybe Hillbilly Corner? Ocean Eleven, right? What you like smiled in his ear and sat back clasping the back of his neck to size him up. -Handsome, soooo handsome. How come you wear no uniform? Oh, IIII know. It's ok, you want drink? Told her he had one coming, ordered her one as she looked over at her friends and cut the smile an inch, but it came back with her drink and talking and singing and clapping with the now thrashing band and the beer sweat poured while they danced, fell in love, lied, felt in their pockets for more money and sometimes came across a wedding ring amongst the change. A Third Class Sonarman became deeply entrenched in a quiet conversation with his chick concerning a great battle that didn't happen. Chicks were everywhere, under the table, on the table, sitting on glasses with frightened spindly feet. One Lance Corporal had one perched on his head trying to down a beer without losing it. More beer, dancing and the hours wore on. There were off-to-the-side conversations about eating out this chick or that chick right on the table and just when it appeared Davies' chick, Suzy was a likely candidate, a balloon man stuck a wide mouth of gold teeth between the outcome.

Why everybody bought all kinds of wonderful blue yellow red balloons and white ones with blue ones inside and he gathered up his cache, was gone. For what must have been three minutes, everybody sat still looking at one another stupidly as the balloons rose from fingers and backs of chairs six feet above them. More beer, the band began again, this time "Dixie," "The Marine Hymn," "Anchors Away," "We Gotta Get Outta This Place," "Sock It To Me Baby" and somebody stuffed a baby chick in one of the girls' drinks. Frowns, then howling laughter when the embarrassment faded, then all the guys were stuffing baby chicks in drinks and snapping their little necks, it was so loud you couldn't hear the cheeps and before long all the baby chicks were dead dying soaked or tied to lingering balloons released and flying high above them, bouncing here, there, against each other on the ceiling dumbly turning round and round the strings around their necks and that band let it rip until the room was so loud the Shore Patrol passing outside came up to have a look.

One of them whispered to the bouncer who shrugged his shoulders.

-Full house.

Packed house fucked-up drunk and stumbling among chairs dancing feet and themselves as the dead chicks danced on the ceiling slowly in smoke until it was all too tired and time to take a chick to a hotel, find one to strap before midnight or something and the vacant looks in their eyes increased in the last couple for the road sloshing down to bellies into the urinals and out to the still thick heat of Olongopo City to be forgotten in lead sleeped hangovers before waking next to perfumed hair and cool thin sheets and as Davies was about to leave, a man began walking around carrying a broom with a nail through the handle popping all the balloons, bringing the dead baby chicks swiftly to the floor to be quietly swept into a pile and put out back. Could be worse jobs, he thought.

-One of the worst.

Camping Out

It was a steel blue night with the stars securely plugged in. He swung the neck of the clam back then forward and let go, listened for the click beneath the water in the bucket and the sound of rising bubbles, broke a thick suction on the camper door and stepped up using the shotgun for leverage. The smell of gunpowder mixed with propane and left-over chicken gave him a tremendous feeling of satisfaction. Ann's hair tumbled from the sleeping bag over the cab and Freddy's bag humped in the middle at her feet. Suddenly it was warm. His eyes worked very hard to accustom themselves to the light. When they came into focus he put the shotgun in the small wooden closet next to the door, closed the door and sat down at the table.

Fifteen minutes later he was still sitting with his arms folded and his jacket on staring at the chicken carcass on the drainboard. He thought he might like a beer, or some coffee, or maybe a glass of red wine, but no matter how he conjured up some reason for moving, he kept thinking he shouldn't. Then he heard it, far off at first, but getting closer. What was it? Some song he'd heard, but there was no radio on. He'd *heard* it before. For chrissakes am I dreaming? He looked out of the corner of his eyes and there she was. How in hell did she get in here. Oh, she was beautiful, in her long transparent gown and lovely blond hair careening easily over her shoulders and those eyes. That mouth and those green eyes, why she was, why it was her singing. She was singing *Summertime*. How did she get in here? He hoped Ann didn't wake up. Impossible. She raised her arms to receive him, but he still couldn't believe it. What the hell was she doing there? Yeah, what?

He'd worked hard to keep his family together, taking care of the kid and taking care of Ann when she was sick. A dream, that's it, a dream. He'd worked damn hard. And that bastard had tried to steal a clam. He deserved a dream, dammit. He needed a dream. His own dream. And there she was right there waiting for him. He tried to straighten his tie and remembered he didn't even have a suit on. She didn't seem to care. Whoever she was just smiled. He'd pay her back right now. For her past, why he'd shove it right down her throat with baby food and soft words. He'd buy her kid's milk, he'd take the kid to the movies while she went to the hospital looking for a way out of her history. And the bastard stole his clam. Came right up to the camper, from god knows where, and took it. Rock salt knocked him out. The sun wouldn't be up for hours and she was there waiting. Oh, he had to get up and kiss this wonderful woman singing to him. She wanted him.

He wanted to tell her he was a puppy dog, he wanted to eat gumdrops by the blue lake and sit in the tall grass with the dream he'd found that never dreamed he was the most beautiful man in the world. And she sang to him in his camper and he found himself humming softly. They'd have children that looked like him and it really would be alright. *His* children. If only he could get up, but Ann and Freddy. He had to protect them, he'd actually shot the bastard, he really didn't want to, it wouldn't kill him, he really didn't want to. He had to do it, to protect his clams and his kid and his wife who was not well. What was this most beautiful girl-of-his-dreams doing? How did she get in anyway? He stood up almost breaking his kneecaps on the table edge and reached for her. She smiled, oh she smiled, he smiled oh he smiled. That bitch, what right did she have to be so beautiful when he had a kid and a sick wife to worry about, where the hell did she get off, anyway?

About the time he'd made up his mind to go for the shotgun Freddy woke up with a nightmare. Ann didn't budge. He had to listen to the little boy tell him word by word, between sighs and tears, about the man with the shaved head and boots who lived in a telephone box and put people on strange tables and shoved boards in their guts and broke all their arms and legs and Daddy, there were arms and legs all over the floor Daddy. They looked like chicken necks with shoes and they was spurtin blood Daddy and this man, this awful man liked to smile and kick 'em Daddy Daddy, he had lots of little bodies he was kickin and cuttin up. I couldn't see him cuttin 'em up Daddy, but they was all over the floor. And then he'd laugh and if one of the bodies he hadn't got around to, ones that was just broken, he'd get real mad and put, he'd pick up the board, he was scary Daddy and then he'd go to sleep laughing and sometimes he'd go to sleep with no clothes on and make funny noises, I can't remember everything, but I was so scared. You won't let that man near me Daddy, will you?

He said he'd fix that mean old man if he tried to hurt him, he might have to hurry, but no. When he turned around she was still there by the door smiling in her long transparent gown, so he asked Freddy if he'd like some milk, the boy said yes and Daddy heated him some milk with much resolution while the most beautiful girl in the world waited for the most beautiful man in the world. He had to finish, he had responsibility, he had to heat responsibility and feed it in small portions to maps. That's it, *maps*. He had to make all the roads fit right, he had to take all the broken bones and put them together somehow. He had to put all those bones together and his wool shirt smelled like hot milk and clam juice. The most beautiful girl in the world would have to wait until he could have his shirt dry-cleaned if he could find the money. No, son, I won't let anyone ever hurt you. Don't worry. He put his glasses on, thinking about the book he'd read when the boy went to sleep, brought the milk in a paper cup, a six ounce paper cup, the boy took sips and the whole trailer smelled like hot milk and wet wool, a heavy breeze turned to gust rumbled against the metal out side, he'd take care of everything.

 He'd put a patch on everybody's dead aunt's grave and they'd all thank him, they'd be oh so happy, he'd show them, he'd put a patch on it and show them. You didn't have to cover up everything completely even if you wanted to, that bastard stole my clam, I hope he's alright, see later. Now son you go to sleep. It'll be alright I promise. And she'd have to wait until he pushed every empty wheelchair in the world and stood by every sick bed and wiped the shit off every asshole because he knew how and he cared, he really cared. And filled all the potholes in the world with his good luck, before she could really sing.

 She looked at him and smiled, oh she smiled and somewhere down there, just below his diaphragm he almost went for it, but his son had finished the milk and the cup was hanging precariously from his little fingers as he began to doze off. Daddy took his big hand and removed the cup, patted the boy's soft fluffy head and put the cup in the plastic bag, inside a plastic bag full of beercans, an empty fifth of brandy and chicken bones sitting next to an empty cardboard case of Budweiser by the door, carefully turned the water on to soak the pan and thought he really ought to heat some water for coffee.

Who was that sonofabitch? Where did he come from? If only she'd stay sleeping, she never slept this well. If only she'd get a good night's sleep once, maybe he could get a good night's sleep. Some day he wouldn't have to be nice all the time. He could sleep too and everything would be alright. Daddy everything would be alright. God dammit go away. She was smiling. Go away, she was singing, she was coming towards him. Oh, most beautifuls, most beautifuls, most beautifuls.

And he looked up at the sleeping boy and began telling him about when he was a pioneer, how he wore a coonskin cap and how he found the lost tribe and how small they were, but how tall they stood and how their feet and toes were spread over the earth and how that was so important because they could center their weight and how he gave them a bag of trinkets for their children and how they thanked him because he didn't ask for anything and how he found the Ocean one day when he was walking and how big and important the Ocean was. And strong, it was so strong and there were lots of funny fish in the deep parts and since he'd found the Ocean other people had made it dirty. It wasn't nice to have to look at a dirty Ocean and everybody should pray for all that dirt to go away and for the Indians. Everybody should pray. She just stood by the door listening, no she was still singing and the wind blew like a sail, yes like a sail outside.

He told his son that being a pioneer was hard work, that you had to work hard to be a pioneer and once you were one, you could really know about the Indians and the Ocean. He wished he was in a sleeping bag, he wished he was a little boy with fluffy hair. If he was a little boy, he'd keep the big bad men who lived in telephones out of his dreams and he'd protect Daddy. He'd be a pioneer for his Daddy and make sure Daddy got warm milk and make sure Mommy wasn't sick all the time, he'd show all the other kids what it was like. There'd be pretty girls all around him when he grew up. Lots of pretty girls.

She was still singing that God Damn *Summertime* when Ann rolled over and asked him if he was alright, was Freddy alright and who was he talking to and what was he doing, why was he up, why didn't he come to bed. He told her to just get a good night's sleep, he had to clean the pan, she rolled over and went back to sleep and he cleaned the pan.

She Was Always Sunday

Naked and falling fifteen stories at three in the morning. A Siamese cat howled from an eighth floor balcony when she passed. She sat bolt up on the couch screaming, "You bastard, you messed up the tv. If you fucked up my TV...!" The room hung familiar silence around her, the only sounds being her breath and a car that seemed to inhale as it drew closer and exhale as it passed down the off-ramp and up the block.

She was armpits stuck to blouse, unnerving black slacks tangled at crotch, sweating panty hose, short hair matted like a rooster, she only drank beer breath, cigarettes and a half-eaten piece of banana cream pie. The pack was strewn all over the floor and when she found a cigarette that was intact, she tapped it unmercifully on the end table before sticking it in her face. Where the hell was the lighter? He probably stole it. Fucked up the tv even if he did have good teeth. Light on the stove. The smoke rose and lingered in the dim yellow light and she shivered with the dream, walked back to the couch and followed the cord. It was intact.

They came and went by the dozens, middle of the week men who smiled and went home early, dazzled with drink and stories of wonderful columns of figures that came out just right, price indexes rising and falling, dockets lost and found, new suits, cars, clubs, wives and a vacant acceptance when she lied about her age. "Who the hell lies about their age anymore? I do." The room had nothing to contribute.

Weeks passed, telephones rang, teeth were brushed, armpits shaved twice a week, she shopped her lunch, bought something, cigarettes, went back to work, left late, intended to marry, but no children thank you. Fifteen floors plenty to think about, the long rushing elevator, one voice beyond her own, all that was necessary as long as it echoed nicely.

She smiled to herself and ran her free hand through her hair, frowned, flicked the ashes on the table, stood up and undressed quickly. "Oh the men, the men." The room seemed hot when she looked down at herself. Bells were ringing somewhere. Somewhere doorbells rang and tennis rackets thwacked morning oppressively.

Tall, black hair, couldn't tell the eyes for the glasses. He'd already had a few drinks when she sat down next to him. Smelled wool, nice guy, bought her a drink right off, then another and another. "I'm worried about not putting on weight." Told her she looked fine, asked her the usual, bought a third and one for himself.

Thrown over the balcony, poor little body broken on the street, cars slowing down, someone found her, was screaming, blood trickling from her nice little mouth, eyes rolled back. Poor girl opened a beer, went back to the couch, flicked on the tv and waited, sipping quietly, waiting. . . .The shadows escaped slowly. She hadn't turned on the sound, but she knew it was something about God. He wasn't loud. Polite, clean, complimentary, probably a genius, it was Sunday, he was a fool. Something poured out of magazine ads and gin bottles, to be petted, fucked, picked up after and thrown away. Her teeth itched.

Someone would have to call her mother. Tell them anything Mother. Tell them she was a career girl, a lawyer. Didn't have time for that. Why look at the place she lives in. What nice people. Safe. Tell them Mother. Oh my poor dear. We had crab at Thanksgiving, just the two of us. Right at that window. That window. It just couldn't have been suicide.

The beer burned. To be talked about, run around with the next door neighbor, whipped over coffee, smiled at, loved, allowed to look around, told what he was doing. Allowed. He stopped in the kitchen and looked in the drawer under the sink, cocked his head, scrutinized. Allowed. Oh yes, he'd drag her to Barbados to look at the moon, or Ohio, New Jersey, somewhere, to meet someone. They always want you to meet someone if you look right. She'd be good to have around if he was drunk and couldn't drive, she wasn't about to. All she had to do was run her tongue over her upper lip for about a minute and any old friend of his would give them a lift.

"Where'd she fall from?" The officer looked up, tipped his hat back on his head and scratched just above his left temple. The gold cap on his right incisor caught the sun.

"I don't know, I just can't, don't know. She was just right there when I came by to the market. Awful, just awful, she's so beautiful. My god. Just going to get some milk."

"Take it easy lady." He readjusted his cap and put his hand on her shoulder. She was all wrapped up in coat and buttons, shopping bag, blue hair and bifocals. So small, so small and tired, she didn't deserve to see this. "Wally, call the wagon and take a walk over to the office and ask around. I'll stay with them. Funny?!"

Real funny ran over the broken cigarettes on the floor and wound up at her lips when she lifted the glass. Her nipples swelled and she smiled. Good hips, thin good hips, enough flesh so he'd like it and still feel the bone underneath. Her skin settled easily through ten o'clock, stretched eleven, tingled eleven-ten, her oh-so-baby-brown-eyes blinked slowly. Noise on the tv. Impossible.

Did he want anything to eat? There was nothing to drink. Next to her. First the usual cuddle, then short pecking on the cheek. Hands off so far. Tried the tongue. Let him sweat. No patience. Hard as a rock, drunk as a loon. Mammy's little boy love shortnin' shortnin', ran down her left nostril and sneezed on his shoulder. "Turn on the tv, will you?" He smiled and turned on the tv. "I haven't gotten a table for it yet." He went to the kitchen and came back with a towel, folded it in half and placed it neatly at the end of the table. When he picked the tv up, it went black.

"I hope you haven't broken it." She yawned. "I hope you haven't broken my television."

"It'll be fine, just fine. Give me a minute."

"Well I'm going to the bathroom while you play electrician."

"It'll be fine." He was crawling around behind the couch.

They come and go, electricians, carpenters, amateur photographers, tv repairmen. All the same. Finger in the hole, ass in a mess. She curled up in Sunday beer and smiled to herself. It was getting chilly. Was the sun shining? Maybe he could fix her bicycle. She could fix it herself. Good hands for a big man. Generally huge hands flop. Flop around. On me. Stick it here. Stick it. Fumbler. Stick it here. I'll smile.

The tv was working. A movie she'd seen. "Good thing."

"What?"

"It works. It's working."

"Told you."

"Good thing." She flopped on the couch and lit a cigarette.

"What the hell are you getting nasty for?"

"Don't get upset."

"What's the big thing? It works."

Condescending she thought. "Oh don't be so sensitive."

Walked around behind her. Room thick in a split second. Warning bell. Between me and the door. A rush. Hot. A nut. A nut in the apartment. "Forget it, you're too sensitive."

"Too sensitive, too sensitive. What's the stink over the stupid tv?"

Light a cigarette. He's going to kill me. Strangle me. With the tv cord. The towel. Panty hose. Has them in his jacket pocket. Taking them out. So warm and slow. Jesus. "Sit over here." She patted the couch next to her left thigh. Fool. "Don't panic."

"Don't panic," he yelled. "DON'T PANIC!"

"Keep your voice down." All around. Remember the smell. Some kind of musk. In case, just in case. He's everywhere. Laughing. He's laughing at me. He's out of his. . .Don't turn around. . .No. . .Please. . .I'm. . ."

The room was getting bright. She took another beer from the refrigerator, let the door swing shut by itself, tossed the cap in the garbage and walked slowly towards the window, pulled the drapes, slid the glass door open and stepped out on the balcony. The sun was stuck in afternoon and the cool breeze made goosebumps leap furiously. She took a swig, held it in her mouth for a good two seconds and leaned against the railing. A yellow pickup was coming down the off-ramp. It was barely moving.

Well Annyyyywaaaayyy

"My father's in town for New Years. I'm going to seeee him, not my real father, I told you that didn't I? Annnyyywaaay." Her eyes dropped to the table briefly, picked up the pieces of the second, embraced the smoke and the murky ceiling, flicked the ashes carelessly on the table and took a dutiful sip of brandy. "Anyway, I won't see him anymore. My real father. I told him last time I wasn't...I mean after the last time. But father is going to beeeee here. I have to see him. He called the hotel. You'd love him. He's huge, he comes up to...Anyway, he left a message and I'm going to see him tomorrow. Would you like to meet him?"

"Oh, my real father? Oh, he just wants to fuck me. That's the only reason he wants me around. The last time, the last time...I mean, I was home, my mother was sick and he came over to Betty's and picked me up and said she was sick. I was strung out, just fucked. And annnyyywayyy, the next thing ya know I'm on this beach and then, and then, he took me up to the canyon and fucked me. I told him no, but I was so strung out. I couldn't, you know. Heee, I don't wanna do that anymore. It's fucked, it's weird ya know. Ya know what I mean? I had enough. My grandfather when I was six or five, something like that and my mother pretending. I walked outta this room, and we lived in this, in this just fucked, fucked place in East L.A. Everybody was strung out, my father bringing all these old fuckers home and listening to jazz. I hate jazz. And my mother, I went into the living room and two of these fuckers were nodded out on the floor and I said, and I said, 'GRANDPA FUCKED ME.' I screamed it. 'GRANDPA FUCKED ME GRANDPA FUCKED ME GRANDPA FUCKED ME.' Nobody even cared.

My mother didn't say anyyything. She didn't say a word, like it didn't even haaapppen.

"Bill, I'll talk to you in awhile, ok? I'm talking to somebody else now. Ok, you go over there and I'll talk to you in awhile.

"Annnyyywayyy, I don't care about fucking. It's like eating ya know. I like ta, ta have guys look at my butt. I love it, I feel like I belong, ya know. But the fucking. My father waited til I was twelve, no thirteen I think. I was goin with this, this Hell's Angel, ya know the kind. He was dumb, god he was dumb. He couldn't even read or write, but I loved him so much. I still love him. He was one, is one of my true, great TRUE loves. I hate smoking, but, I just hate it, don't know why, but anyway my real father just came into my room one night and well we fucked. It wasn't that big a thing. I just said well, what the hell and it was, I mean I was so fucked up all the time anyway. It was after I came over, came back home I mean. I ran away from home so many times and I went to this, to this. I didn't know anything. AANY-THING and met these guys and they took me to their place somewhere and they gave me acid. I never took acid before ya know and this one guy, this one guy, well he came over, I heard this music ya know. Wow, I didn't know WHAT it was and I said what's that. I asked him what it was and he said it was a Ravi Shankar, at least I thought he said that. I said, 'What's a Ravi Shankar.' I guess he told me cuz I started running all around, all over the house yelling, I was screaming 'I WANT A RAVI SHANKAR. I WANT A RAVI SHANKAR!' Isn't that a trip? But I got fucked. I don't know how many times and I finally passed out and then, and then, I escaped and I was in some section of L.A. I didn't know. I dunno. I finally did get home and my mother was so nice. And she said, 'Oh you poor beebbbee' and she gave me a bath and put me to bed, but my father fucked me all the time ya know, they kept, well he kept moving all over, in and out. She's a waitress and I just don't care now. I care, but well anyway. My stepfather's in town and I'm going to see him.

"Why are you looking at me like that? I love brandy. Nooooo, not him. That's Bob. He's a musician. Anyway, I woke up and felt this thing, this thiiing on my butt and I just got up and told him no, I've had enough of that. Oh Bob? He's just a friend. You know. We talk now and then, but Bob was funny. Remember when you and me? Remember we tried to pick up these sailors? Bob and I were sitting over there on the couch with Don and Evvie drinking and this guy, this guy came in and he said ya mind if I sit down and do some coke and IIII said well sit right down and well Bob's face turned red. It was crazy, the music was. Caruso, and he sat down and took out this teeny teeny gold spoon and we, well, he kept shoving it under my nose and finally I had to take his hand and swing it over to Bob's nose and we sat there. Finally he left and we went over to Matt's house for a drink. It was the same night I guess. I guess that was another night with the sailors. Remember? Menage Á Trois Menage Á Trois? We almost brought home the whole French Navy. That one sailor was sooo cute wasn't he? You wouldn't let me bring him home, I guess you wouldn't, but anyway, after we left, we were going over to Bob's, after Matt's and it was about three thirty and he had this old radio of mine, under his arm. I was moving, and a can of mushroom soup under his arm too and we were thinking about coke. You know how that is. And who do ya think we run into? Riiiight. The coke freak and his friend and Bob says to play up to him and maybe we can score. The one guy leaned on me and kept askin if we had any dust. Bob didn't know what dust was, but anyway, they ended up wantin us ta go, ta go to Oakland and they said we'd get some coke there, but Bob decided to get out of it because he said they'd rape me. He was probably right, but anyway. When we got to Kearny and Pine, one of the guys, he was poppin downers, flagged this car down and the next thing ya know these guys jump outta the car and kick the shit outta these coke freaks. And we ran, we ran right down the middle of the block and around the corner on Bush and up the alley. Belden Alley, by the Temple hotel. I was worried Bob might drop my radio. It was a trip. Then we, well, we walked home almost.

"We got to the East Bay Terminal and Bob got the idea they might come there if they was goin to Oakland. We were so high, he just knew they would, so we sat around the Terminal with that hunger. And we waited and waited. We took pictures of ourselves in the booth. We thought we were so cool. You should've seen the pictures. Wait. Wow, you wanna see the pictures? Oh, I thought I had 'em in my purse, but annnyyywaaayy, we waited til five-thirty and they never came. It was really far out. Nothing happened. We're just friends ya know.

"Oh, ya know what we had to do? We took the cats up to Coit Tower. It was soooo sad. All those poor kittys. We even brought some food up there, but they went after a couple weeks. I hate smoke. Something to do.

"Hey, but ya know this guy from Seattle. . . ?"

Ambulance

The pavement blistered, cars levitated on white heat, buses droned through boiling oily jelly slapping their doors every block or so, hands full of crumpled lunch bags moved towards ashcans and gutters, corned beef sandwiches and gin churned in tummies on all the elevators everywhere and somebody's secretary for the American Cancer Society stepped in the Lady's Room at the downstairs level of the office on James street to see if the perspiration under her arms showed too much the afternoon began.

Flies skirted the pools in the parks, kids smelled like bathing suits chlorine baseball dirt sneakers and grass, popsicles melted, salads for supper sprung up in housewives' heads, our siren caught the air by surprise at the four-hundred block of Salina. I turned the oxygen up to twelve when her face went ashen thinking J. Bell was probably adjusting his forever blue tie, smoothing back the thinning black hair, flexing his right arm to get that white starched cuff from the low button on the air-conditioning to the phone, to call Webb Booter on Townsend, to see if Wendall Funeral still wanted to buy the 1958 Buick hearse I couldn't afford at the time.

Tans were long since browner than expected, great sexy days were cooking to hot slippery-bellied nights with splashes of musk turning heads all over town. It was powerful enough to keep dogs confused and panting and with that kind of heat you were pumping life for everything it was worth, blessing fans, damning meter maids, leaning on your forearm or passed out bonkers.

A huge rollicking fat man with red hair and enormous green eyes took his suitcase down from the rack while the bus driver tossed his hat on the dash and wound the sign back to New York. By the time he was finished the fat man had ambled on down to the Men's Room to splash cold water on his forehead. He unbuttoned the top two buttons of his white short-sleeved shirt with the green and yellow parrots perched all over it, wiped his chest hair with a paper towel that didn't seem to do much good, bared his thick teeth, picked a piece of Kraft American Cheese from the left incisor, smiled at himself said "Polish muh knob" three times, "It's a helluva place" I've heard, unbuckled the khaki pants flapped his shirt tail a couple of times and smoothed them around a gargantuan waist, while the dollar-an-hour wino Pedro O'Hara had hired to hold the ladder shifted uneasily, trying to figure out whether or not Pedro, who was mumbling about brushes and the fact he couldn't reach the eave without moving the ladder, could, or would notice if he let go with one hand to pull *his* pants up.

In Thorden Park a Monarch butterfly just laid back in the humidity and *hoped*, paper pickers swung their sticks lazily, missing dixie cups, empty cigarette packs and butts with great abandon. Empty beer cans didn't stand a chance. Barry Weinberg checked the gray at his temples, slid into his sandals, plucked the Camels into the pocket of his blue chambray shirt, eased the eighty-five dollar flamenco guitar out of the corner and went out on the front porch to play the only three chords he knew, Pedro confided to himself that he didn't know anything as he climbed down the ladder with a prayer in his left prefrontal lobe and a cold beer running around his forehead. Larry Segal and Fred the Tail Gunner stood in separate lines waiting to cash their disability checks, Jerry Kline grinned the movie grin, slid a Steinbrau across the bar of the Orange Cafe, slapped Wally Meyer's forty cents in the till and went back to his fourth IPA of the day. He had two rounds of golf on his mind and when Wally asked for a pack of matches, he sunk a twelve foot putt. Bob Dylan was making a five year leap across the charts, but you couldn't feel the wind that day.

I told Al she wasn't going to make it, he stepped on it, tossed *his* hat on the dash, clicked the mike button three times, who the hell was it beating on my yesterday door that I never answered. I'd slipped down the stairs and listened to see if I could recognize the breathing, the sheets stuck together, the bathtub was dirty, I hoped she wouldn't be back, I hoped it wasn't a recruiting officer, I hoped the old gal on the litter pulled through, it was too nice a day to die.

Thick necks sweated in wrinkles, part-time civil rights lawyers hung on parking meters dreaming of rare roast beef sandwiches, root beer and a palm on the butt of one of those so fiiiine sociology ladies wagging past dreaming their dream of saving those poor souls. "Picket God," somebody said when the six-toed Lady talked about Selma, had to get arrested without Wally Meyer's help. "Might hurt her," he said out loud when she passed the bar window. "Not what you're talkin' bout," somebody said when he half turned around.

Art Kleps drank coffee in the second booth on the left just inside the door of the Savoy Restaurant on Marshall Street with its precious laundries drinking steins sweaters sweatshirts shoes shorts belts bras double-parked corvettes milkshakes toothbrushes bermuda shorts occasional berets Beethoven beer Late Satre and Jesus Later. He watched the traffic and the lawn in front of the parking lot next to the stone University Hospital that took up the rest of the block. He watched the German Shepherd sweating on the grass and the bodies coming and going lying down in halters and shorts, getting up to watch and he clicked away the unmaking of many beds, the making of many virgins and the founding of the Neo-American Church. He'd be the Chief Boo Hoo, but today had a Boo Hoo of its own and it had its best punch stuck right in the sky.

Betty Wimple rolled over when the sun threatened to fry her in bed, rubbed her eyes thinking everything stuck to everything, there was crust on her pubic hairs and skids on the sheets and Pedro O'Hara's dog was down the hall drinking all the toilet water he could. Fred Wolfert bought fifty pounds of potatoes deciding he could feed everybody including himself potato salad, Ben May adjusted his wire-rimmed glasses, shook his head at the floor thinking that was a helluva lotta mayonnaise.

"Too hot," Pedro said to the Wino.

"D.O.A.," I wrote in the book.

"Celery," Wolfert said to May who was shaking his head at the grocery cart.

Mr. Blue put on his battered fedora, asked his seventeen and a half inch mongrel with no teeth if he was hungry and prepared a note with hex signs on it for Wolfert's door. Frank Morrow stared through the one and a half inch glory hole in the Maxwell Tea Room and waited for the guy to sit down, while It sweated hissed loved smoked, children played Tarzan on a rope hung from an elm by Jamesville Reservoir, the Herald Journal prepared a photo essay around fountains, fans, summer dresses, swimming pools, outside sandwiches, drenched handkerchiefs and night workers escaped into afternoon movies. Policemen looked surprisingly cool in their short sleeved shirts, an overweight whore in a green cotton dress peeked under a shade on the second floor of somewhere, and asked no one in particular what time it was. The Brown Fox considered his sickle cell, but breathed the good breath in the consistent boil, my uniform was soaked in sweat and death beyond me next to me. It was a matter of chance foolishness disbelief belief patience impatience defiance. Just plain not thinking about it sang it ate it fucked it bled it drank it, the sun would come up, we'd be on the roof with a jug at dawn to watch, I had to get a standby somehow "OOOOOOOOOeeeeee," Al said to Rosie, who hadn't gotten out of bed when we pulled into the morgue parking lot, "OOOOOOOOOEEEEEEEEEE!"

And I was off listening to someone whistling Sometime in the street below my third story window, hidden by an elm so I couldn't see who it was, unless I waited til he passed to my left beyond the roof of the first floor porch to the bright grass and sidewalk, but he didn't come that way after all, and kept on singing (where was it coming from?). Barry Weinberg's guitar plunked the same three chords as yesterday, I let the Japanese beads slap carelessly, and opened the 1932 G.E. refrigerator with the motor on top that ground like mad on hot days, and took out a dish of last night's macaroni and hamburg, a Steinbrau, put the little pan of the big and little pans on the stove, dumped in the macaroni, lit off the burner and rubbed my sweaty toes together, lifting one leg and then the other to see how much dirt had collected on the soles of my feet from all that pacing, took a good belt of beer and wondered if the Brown Fox would shave my head for me like he did last summer, kissed last year's Lynn for the fourth time, looked for this moment's woman, and settled into the straight back chair by the window, listening for music, burning macaroni, the shallow swish in the can, announcing another, and the hush and smile of being damn glad to have a loft for sixty a month.

"Keep her covered up," Al said when I swung the back door open.

"What for?"

The shuffleboard puck hung between dings in the air conditioned Orange, Wally walked around to pull it out from under, setting his beer on the bar, and the outside flies skated aimlessly in the thick air by Wolfert's closed window. He wasn't thinking time, except perhaps the money it would take to get his Crosly Hotshot back on the track at Watkins Glen and he wasn't worried about Mr. Blue. After all, he'd painted the door a nice shade of black, which was one of the reasons Mr. Blue attached the note to it, on the way to the market, he'd complained about the Indian students upstairs, who he said dried their socks in the oven, and then it was Willy the downtrodden cocksucker who cried in his sleep, the rent was due, Rosie was leaning a little hard on the domestic side of the place, she didn't live in, he'd have to tell Al where the hell that was at. Ben May wasn't leaning on anything in particular, just peeling potatoes with a mad grin on his face, thinking a short rainstorm about five wouldn't hurt.

Two doors up, on the shady downhill corner of South Crouse and East Adams, cattywampus from the *GET ANYTHING YOU WANT FOR YOUR COLD ANYTIME DRUG STORE COLD OR NOT,* Wanda pulled one leg out from under the last remnant of a tucked in sheet, scratched her head with one hand and tossed the beer can at the ten gallon garbage pail sitting at the foot of the bed next to the window opening onto a very wide front porch, with the other. It bounced off the rest, slid back between the bed and rolled off somewhere underneath, made a slight turn where the floor warped, picked up speed coming back, hit the edge of the kitchen door to her left and settled in until cleaning time which, "Was a long time comin," she said out loud. "Where did that man go?" It was twenty past one by the Orange Cafe clock and Larry Segal swung the unpredictable doors in the right direction he thought, peeled off five, said hello to everyone and a couple of people who weren't there, said "Aria" to Wally's crossword puzzle, Wally said, "I know," Betty Wimple climbed into her own shower, Pedro stuck his head in his back hallway and called the dog sleeping by the toilet and I took the receipt from the morgue attendant, stuck it in the back of the book, Fred The Tail Gunner bumped into Mr. Blue at the meat counter on the way to the beer cooler, Al ten-foured a 78 possible drowning at Onondaga Creek, flipped the siren on and was halfway out of the lot before I caught up.

"A drowning?"

"I think so."

"I hate drownings."

"Not anymore than hangings."

"About the same. How's Rosie?"

"Rosie's Rosie. Gots ta get off a here by four. We'll whip this one into Crouse Irving and I'll stop by the house and call her, if the Wolf ain't home." He cocked his head and swept a huge arc with his hand that bounced off the ceiling of the rig. "Be glad this ain't a Volkswagen, barely get muh legs under the dash now."

The Herald Journal put a hold on for the drowning, Jerry Kline got in his stationwagon leaving Wally behind the bar. Mr. Blue paid seventy-three cents for a piece of top round, I took the Brooks out of the bag and tested it, the ball fluttered madly and the rig slipped across East Adams and Salina, slowed for the dip on the West Adams side, swung around a laundry truck, Al leaned on the siren, my yesterday's door knocked again, I rounded up the last four and half pieces of macaroni, stuffed them in, reached for the beer and sat back watching the traffic careen behind us and thought J. Bell was probably due to tell the dispatcher he was going to take a late lunch.

Frank Morrow decided it was too hot in the tea room, but perked his ears when the door opened sighing, "What's a mother to do?" Somebody's little blond three year old girl took a playful swipe at the Monarch and almost fell in the rose bush before Mamma grabbed her and the lifeguard at the pool across the hill blew his whistle furiously.

The Lady's Home Journal in the Planned Parenthood waiting room took the weight of Betty Wimple's purse without fanfare and I stuck my finger in the little girl's mouth, hooked a huge chunk of something, flipped it on the bank and turned her head to the side. She coughed weakly and seemed to get more cyanotic by the second.

"How old?"

"I'd say seven." I looked at her little hands.

"What?" It was a different voice. I heard Al wheeling the litter over.

"Six maybe seven," I repeated.

The fireman in charge asked us which hospital, we slid the litter in back, it caught right away and clicked in. "Crouse Irving." I hopped in back, started working the Brooks and almost fell over backwards when Al floored it. "She gonna make it?"

"Cheyne-Stoking."

"American Eight, you're cleared for Crouse Irving."

"Ten-four on the way to Crouse Irving."

The chunks began clogging the airway. "I could do with a transfer," I hollered between exhales. I remembered it was supposed to be my off day. She might make it, I thought. We got the junk out. Just keep it even, come on little girl, it's a helluva nice day. Come on. I watched her tummy.

By the time Wanda rubbed her eyes into focus and saw the shape she was in cluttering the bathroom mirror, Two had passed the window and was on the way to Two O Three looking for a piece of shadow to lie under. She mussed up her pageboy, pulled down the corner of her left lower eyelid, examined the eye for redness, cocked her head, tried to look up her nose, tried to let up the shade that some one had written on in lipstick,
HI
I AM A
DUCK
all the way, but settled for DUCK, turned on both faucets, picked a washcloth out of the bathtub behind her and washed another four minutes off her face. She mooed into it several times and asked herself where that sonofabitch had gone, brushed her teeth without toothpaste, went at the armpits with the washcloth, dried them, and Cane Foster, the night bartender at the Orange fucked her for one hour on a brass bed with a single lightbulb hanging over it, while she rolled on the Ban. They rolled over, she got on top when the front screen door slammed announcing the arrival of the phone bill and by two-thirty, she was dressed in loose jeans, a pair of faded pink zories, had successfully sucked him off a second time, found a cigarette next to the sugar bowl on the kitchen table and a beer in the fridge and was in the process of opening it when Mr. Blue's dog began yipping at his feet on the sidewalk out front. He decided God was punishing him with all that heat and adjusted his fedora.

We pulled into the lot and she seemed to be doing a little better. Some of the cyanosis had faded and she showed a slight touch of breathing on her own. I had to keep at it, Al was screaming "fucking asshole" at a green cab with no driver parked in front of the emergency room door. There was no time to look him up, the doctor wasn't waiting for us, so we parked right in the middle of the lot and I carried her in. It wasn't too surprising to find out they didn't know we were coming. She was cold as late September, I was having a helluva time doing mouth-to-mouth on a dead run, *WOULD SOMEBODY GET OFF THEIR ASS, THIS LITTLE GIRL MIGHT MAKE DECEMBER.*

Wolfert dumped more potatoes in the sink, Ben May shook his head and kept on peeling, two thirty-three sent the Monarch over by the iris' running a neat row along the side of a paint chipped building to meet a friend on a slow flutter to the bottom of the front porch. The two of them flitted across the small lawn, made a left turn behind the blue sign with orange lettering that said EAST AFRICAN STUDIES, then made for the shade of the bushes on the far side of the lot. Just inside the door Judy Ostrovsky tore another mat out of the typewriter, remembered for some damn reason that she was adopted and yelled upstairs, "Hey, Maaaaaark. You gotta minute?" Her voice almost whined, the sun showed no mercy and worked a steady burn down the middle of the afternoon. Jerry Kline settled for an IPA in the club house.

At 3:04 the six-toed lady leaped in front of a crane at the Urban Renewal site on lower East Adams and was promptly arrested, the Brown Fox overcame a tremendous urge to leave the back porch for some Captain Mac's steamed clams and beer and Wolfie's Famous Chili got no takers at the Savoy. A tall man with silver hair and a smooth blue suit, matching tie, steel gray eyes and a tape recorder made a mental note to forget he tried to stick a poison cigar in Fidel Castro's mouth, and Binghamton, New York, Boston, Roxbury, Connecticut, Auburn, Oswego, Buffalo, Camden, Corning, Manlius, Red Hook, Chevy Chase, Evanston, Groom, Pittsfield, Fonda, Arlington, Amityville, Bennington, Bangor and a few hundred others were thankfully sweating, or not sweating Syracuse, New York in late May.

"Sooooo fiiiine," O'Hara said to the Dog when he held the door of the Orange open. The Dog sauntered in and O'Hara followed, Betty pulled him on top for the sixth time which made him feel much better, since the third time he'd been worried about the fact Pete might not show up to hold the ladder. Al honked to him as we passed, but he didn't turn around. We got a transfer from Syracuse Memorial to Syracuse Community. I sighed and Al pulled over in front of his place to call Rosie. I knew damn well he'd sneak a beer, but was real happy when he brought half of it out in a paper cup for me. "He's home," he said and let the emergency brake off.

"So what?"

"So, I gotta talk to Rosie. Private."

"None a my business."

Al lapsed into dreams of Peyote in San Diego, true love, peanut butter, a Whisperin' Smith Hamburger, all of which he told me about in the short time it took to go around the block, and up to Memorial.

I had to piss, Hank the Bank thought about getting out of the bar business. Lucy Cream Cheese thought she was pregnant, was, and tried to figure out how to corner Al in the Orange. Larry Segal laughed like hell when the Fat Man with the parrots on his shirt bounced off the swinging doors and asked the first girl in the first booth, the only girl in the place, her first time, if he could sketch her for a dollar and a half and "Would anyone spring for a beer? It's one hot mother." The juke box cornered Summer Wine, stuck a needle in it and Nancy Sinatra moaned. Wolfert stirred in the mayo, Ned Kresge stuffed three beans in his craw and washed them down with Spodee, the Fat Man picked the girl's nose to a tee, O'Hara raised the beer over his head and noticed a small mole on the girl's left wrist and shook his head when the Dog started for the table. "It's only four o'clock," he said.

Four-thirty had Al at the back of the stretcher and me at the front. We lifted the dear old thing out of bed while her husband commented on how nice she looked in her new white nightgown. "Why you look just like the Statue of Liberty." When I realized how much she weighed, I managed a smile. "At least a distant cousin," I said.

I'll blow him the first chance I get Wanda said to herself, Judy Ostrovsky stuck to herself and the typewriter, I told the Statue of Liberty she really did look quite nice when we put her in the rig, then I made a quick trip to the head. I stood over the bowl while this strange woman chased me all over her apartment with a butcher knife, out the back door, back in the door, out again. I finally gave her the slip by running up the hall stairs and hanging out the window while she stood right underneath brandishing the knife. I hoped I wouldn't break an ankle, zipped up and wrote WELFARE on my info sheet. I could see the whites of her eyes slashing the night, Fred The Tail Gunner slammed the door on me last month for no apparent reason, The Statue of Liberty told me she'd been married to Horace for thirty-seven years and the Fat Man worked the girl's ear all over his sketch pad.

May was beside himself watching Wolfert stuff the potato salad in the lower compartment of the fridge, Wally wanted to hit me in the mouth, but hadn't figured out how, when or why and Judy was trying to figure out how to straighten out Neal the linguist and Neal called her to get approval from the department on an added Swahili class at four forty-six. The six-toed lady called a lawyer, Betty went into her bedroom and tried to figure out how the damn BC Pac worked, besides her breasts were too small, she thought. The Fat Man told Segal his name was Lawrence of Everywhere, gave the girl a little more eyelash and a wink of his own, Wally began hollering about the way they were treated at the Urban Renewal Site, he'd heard it on the radio, Judy punched Mark's extension button, put a cover on the typewriter and Frank Morrow flushed the toilet for the last time that afternoon.

What the hell to do with the rest of the afternoon just sat on the wrinkled sheets in Pedro O'Hara's bed and seeing there was no one in it, several faces crossed his mind, entertaining him long enough to order another beer. I don't wanna think about it, caught up with him when he pushed the change across the bar, put tomorrow's paintbrush in his hand, and felt in his pocket. He decided he needed a sponsor for the next few rounds and searched the room quickly. The back of Segal's head got five seconds worth of attention.

It was about this time of day that Pakada's spider monkey always managed to unlock the cage and run a number on the hamsters in the box next to the waterheater, next to the catbox just inside the kitchen door. On quiet nights O'Hara swore he heard the monkey raping the hamsters. Sometimes he'd actually lean out his bedroom window and yell downstairs. It was disgraceful he said. Done with hamsters, the monkey'd terrorize the guppies with sweeping plunges of arms into the aquarium, then he'd leap into the middle of the green drapes in the living room just to see if he could tear them down before Pakada got home. Her German shepherd sat on the lawn across from the Savoy waiting for her to get off work so he could get his medicine, that might possibly prevent his shitting the floors from one end of the house to the other. She called him and he came running. They'd stop at the Orange to see if McGuane was there. Maybe he'd like to help her feed the horse. Another wonderful evening of lies and promises. Maybe she'd lose the whole bubble somewhere between her legs. Marriage stamped itself on the back side of her septum and draped apprehension behind each hazel eye when she saw him going in the place ahead of her.

Meter maids shuffled the last few minutes of the shift for as much mileage as they could get, at least several thousand gallons of charcoal lighter began soaking up backyard charcoal and a thousand tons of carbon monoxide surprised the late afternoon with some fine nausea. The sun wasn't about to hang it up, but did settle back a bit. Wolfert rocked in the straight back chair on the porch, pushing it just to the point where he thought it would piss Mr. Blue off if he saw it. The note with the hex sign started a cynical grin that sat on his face for about three minutes, then his thoughts turned to Ben May and Wanda sitting on the steps. She was licking his ear while he tried to read a book. "Can'tcha see I'm busy?" He tried to shake her off. Fred went in the house and came back with a plate of potato salad and two forks. Wanda was tugging on May's tee shirt and he was having one helluva time convincing her he was really reading. Somehow the potato salad ended up half dumped on the book provoking a sharp "GOD DAMMIT, I'm readin'," followed by May's perennial laugh signifying disbelief in most of the things that seemed to happen to him without logic or intent on his part. He almost got mad, backhanded the salad off the book, but completely broke up when Wanda started trying to pick it up. "Don't waste food," Fred smirked. "Only Nicky Hilton wastes food and Nicky Hilton should go to war one year for every day I had to, because he has more to lose." Propped right next to that statement was a lackadaisical paranoia concerning eviction and an urge to kick Mr. Blue's dog even if it didn't have any teeth. Wanda sat on the sidewalk eating and Ben May just watched her, shaking his head from time to time and repeating. "Jesus Christ, I don't believe it." He'd try reading, but the smudges on the book had him going for another hour.

"Yeah, cash." Al hung up. "He's gonna do it. Be in at six."

"I gotta get off my ownself." We walked into the late afternoon with a little sigh of relief. There was a slight breeze trying to get around the corner of the building. I could sense it wasn't going to get to us before we left Community Hospital.

Lawrence of Everywhere couldn't stand the thought of waiting until dark, so he asked Martha as he handed her the sketch, if it might be possible to eat her, which brought a brighter flush to an already superb eastern tan and a little din to her altruism, a surprise trickle of perspiration down her left armpit, into her bra and a half "NO" sneaking through some really fine white teeth, slipping over a wonderfully contrived pout, hitting the sound of the air conditioner so softly Pedro slipped a quarter in the jukebox so she wouldn't embarrass the Dog, who was asleep under the shuffleboard machine. Segal thought about home and supper. Not showing up registered a big yes when it turned five forty-five.

"Wanna come and see the horse?"

"Sure Pak. Have a drink." McGuane came up with his best condescending grin, a wry spread that was angularly handsome, insistently demonic and had a way of infuriating even the most impervious woman.

"No, I gotta feed the animals." She leaned over and patted the Dog's head. Lawrence of Everywhere was making a brief sketch in his mind, the dog gave a lingering fly just under a quarter of a swat with his tail, Marsha agreed to pose again "for free," "for art," Lawrence decided he was very hungry and asked Segal where he could get a good meal. Segal slammed the puck down the alley and "EASY OUT" registered right before his very eyes.

"Naomi, this is Lawrence of Everywhere." She'd just love that. "What we havin for dinner? Oh, chicken cacciatore. And salad." He saw himself clasping his hands in mock domesticity. What an evil grin he thought to himself. Maybe Vic would like Lawrence.

"Why I'd just love to come for dinner. I'll sketch your portrait."

"I'll bet you will."

"Sure you don't want to feed the horses?"

"Later Pak. Have a beer." She sat down and he ordered. She paid.

We let Al off on the corner of East Adams and South Crouse and he ran right into the Pack Rat, as Wolfert called him, who was drinking his eleventh pepsi. Said he had three jobs and when Al asked him why three jobs, he said it was because he couldn't find another one. I asked Brett if he knew anybody else who might like to work that night. We got an 80 in East Syracuse before he could answer. "Lemmie think about it," he said about halfway down the block. I pulled the brim of my hat over my eyes and leaned back. Brett proceeded to tell me one of his more audacious fuck stories.

Martha waddled around upstairs in the Orange wiping off whatever tables needed wiping, grumbling to herself and wincing every few steps. The huge back brace stuck to her shoulders and greased her thick sides under the white uniform making everything stick at the point where pain and heat meet as invincible odds. Downstairs the jukebox drowned out Pakada's waning argument, Wally closed the door to the phonebooth and dialed the City Jail, Pedro asked McGuane for a loan, Segal asked Lawrence where he was from and Al got a goose from Wanda on the front porch and a plate of potato salad shoved in his hands in the kitchen.

Park pools emptied, lawn sprinklers sputtered, the news announced, Little Diane Nadeau narrowly escaped death by drowning early this afternoon and is reported in critical condition at Crouse Irving Hospital, people who didn't have air conditioning pulled up their shades, tv screens flashed pretty girls, older women fanning themselves, outside lunches, handkerchiefs wiping laborer's brows, butterflies in the park, flowers, predictions of more to come, nurses showered and as the sun lingered above Onondaga Lake catching the corners of the buildings without surprise, John Breckinridge, having worked himself through a trigeminal rhizotomy, four months on hypothermia with a body temperature of eighty-six degrees, loss of house, job, and use of left hand, pulled the sheets away from his body, held the catheter straight up and asked the nurse who was feeding him what she thought of that, then screamed so loud, the security guards in the parking lot four floors down were sure it was real. "HELP HELP HELP GET THE SHERIFF,

GET THE SHERIFF, I'M BEING MURDERED...HELP HELP."

Cane Foster got off the bus at East Genesee and South Crouse and Wanda sat on the porch in front of her place waiting. We passed more reasons than I wanted to think about for getting a standby, I had to get off. J. Bell signed the bill of sale for the hearse, we came to a screeching halt next to a tricycle and a little boy bloody and crying, American One transferred the Statue of Liberty to her home, she was just as heavy for them and Barry Weinberg's guitar rested in the corner. Barry rested on the single bed next to it.

Alan Ladd Meets the Emigrant From Oakland

A woomblee bee, a doomblee bee, a honey honey honey honey what'cha bee. Long time comin 'n a long time gone, pickin up whiskers 'n puttin em down. One little man 'n one little frog. A woomblee bee, a doomblee bee, a honey honey honey honeyhoney bee. Well, hullo there. Didn't see ya fur a second. Bin busy with this here lawn chair. How's that? Made it up fur a bed. Folds right out ta a bed. See, the legs come right down. There. I kin adjust the head rest. Put it right up in the park 'n sun muhself. 'N it folds right up. . .like this, so's ya kin carry it. Muh name's Cal, 'n you?

Can't hear too good, but since I got this bed 'n the lamp here. Hooks right on top it does. See here. Say, you know where I kin git 'n extension cord? The way I figger it, have a swig a this. The way I figger, if I kin git up. Ya see over there? The roof on the top a the furniture joint? Figone's I think they call it. It's flat up there. Now if I kin just git me 'n extension cord, I kin git up there 'n plug inta the sign light, see, 'n I kin read. Have ta pull it out by mornin, but I git up early innyway. Might need 'n adapter a some kind. Hummmm. . .Naw, I don't think Figone Hardware. Izzat how ya say it? Sure would be nice. Up there all night readin 'n sleepin in muh new bed. God Damn. Where'd ya say you wuz from? Yeah, go ahead, have some more. I bin inta it too much lately anyway. No, no, go ahead. Me?

Oh, I came over in forty-nine. From Oakland. On the bus. Bin here iver since. Ya see, I used ta walk the horses up ta the paddock over at Golden Gate. Got three dollars a whack. Wuz a livin it wuz, 'n well, one day I had this nag I wuz takin up. Had nine dollars in muh pocket. This guy tells me ta bet the horse. Now I get ta thinkin, well bet five, two ta place, still leaves two 'n one more horse gits me 'nother three. Nuthin ta lose right? So I bets the horse 'n the horse wins. He wins big. I mean BIIIIg. Don't mind if I do. Bigger 'n shit he wins.

Sooooo, I takes the money 'n I git onna bus fur San Francisco 'n on the bus, there's this young lady see. . .She has some books, 'n I start talkin ta her 'n she sez she's in college 'n I sez, 'What'cha doin this evenin?' 'N she sez she's gotta git home, cause her mother will miss 'er. So I sez, 'How'ja like ta go out? Look I got this money. Where would'ja like ta go in San Francisco? The fanciest place ya can think of, 'n I'll take ya there? How's that?'

She starts tellin me 'bout her mother again 'n I sez why don't-cha call her 'n she sez maybe she kin 'n I sez, well sure ya kin 'n she sez she always wanted ta go ta Finocchio's, 'n I sez if that's where ya wants ta go, that's where we'll go. We'll jus git a snack 'n then we'll go, 'n we went. She wuz beautiful 'n afterwards we took care a the other business. Ya know, Finocchio's has quite a show. Quite a thing.

The next day, I wake up on Nob Hill somewhere 'n still got money left. Right. So it's early 'n I jus walk all aroun' San Francisco all day lookin at things. Good town it is.Long bout evenin, I git ta walkin down roun' Broadway 'n Columbus. There wurnt none a them shows like they got now. Some real nice places ya know. 'N there on the corner, on the corner, where that, what is it, Carol Doda place is now, wuz this, this bull dyker. She wuz standin with this beeooootiful thing that, that looked, why she looked jus like Alan Ladd. 'N I thought, now there's somethin, 'n I sez, now I'm gonna make a woman otta her.

Well the first thing I know I gotta do, is ta git ridda the bull dyker. She hedda go. So's I take em both down ta this place on Broadway. Don't evin remember the name, but we git there 'n

I start buyin drinks 'n goin easy on muhself. Pretty soon the bull dyker's gittin drunk see, 'n she goes ta the head see, so I sez ta the girl Alan Ladd, her name turns out to be Monique or Monica, or somethin. I sez, 'Why don'tcha come with me 'n leave her?' Well she don't go fur it at furst, so's I work real fast. Gotta git to 'er fur the bull dyker gits back. I sez, 'Look, yur friend's drunk, kin'tcha see? I promise I won't try nuthin.' 'N she hems 'n haws, but finally she sez ok, jus when I wuz thinkin, Jesus, the bull dyker wuz due back.

We walks aroun' awhile, then I gits a bottle 'n we goes 'n gits a hotel room down roun' Sixth 'n Mission somewhere. Git up there, why wur havin a good ole time, then she gits tired. Begins takin off her clothes 'n when she gits down ta the panties I kin't stand it no more. I jus lose muh control 'n grab 'er. Why she jus lets out the most God awful scream 'n she begins gittin sick 'n screamin all over the place. Yellin fur help 'n shit, when she goes fur the phone, I runs right otta there. Her jus standin there pukin with the panties roun' her ankles, hangin on the phone screamin. Jesus. Well, I forgot muh shoes, I did. Ran right otta there in muh stockin feet. Runnin up 'n down the hall. Kin't find no way out lessen I goes through the lobby. Went down the back stairs, then up the stairs 'n alla time I kin hear her screamin. Finely find this door 'n when I open it, it's 'n exit alright, but there ain't no stairs, jus open space two floors down. 'N somebody's comin. What do I do? Why I jumps.

Broke both ankles I did. There I wuz lyin in the alley. Gawd the pain wuz awful. Felt bad about the girl, but muh ankles hurt so, 'n I realize I kin't walk 'n I don't have no shoes. In those days they'd arrest y iffin ya didn't have shoes on. So I hadda stay in the alley all night. Muh feet got so swollen. Come mornin' I look aroun' 'n manage ta git across the street 'n down the block ta this other hotel. On muh hands 'n knees I wuz. Went up ta the clerk. He wuz gonna have me arrested. I told him I wuz robbed of all muh money, at least most of it 'n iffin he could help me git some shoes so I could walk maybe I could find em. He sez he'll try 'n he puts me in the back room while he looks up some shoes. Found some too.

Come afternoon we call the cops 'n I spend all afternoon ridin roun' with em looking fur the guys that robbed me. Described em pretty well, but well, I, I, we never did find em. By the time muh ankles wuz well I wuz broke 'n couldn't git back across the bridge, cuz ya kin't walk, so I bin here iver since. Ya really otta go ta that Finocchio's. It's the best one ivin now. Say, you sure you don't know where I kin git 'n extension cord?

Sherlock Goes to the Vet

Sherlock sore. Legs ache, lymph nodes hurt, headache, headover cook breakfast, cook everything in house. Eggs, mushroom, sour cream, old clock, desk, one fluid ounce vitamin E oil, seven pieces erasable bond and sock. Make fine omelet, but sore prick.

Ride to Vet, that it, Sherlock Toyota drive. Keep see great posters toy trains and Jaqueline Susann tee shirt. Sherlock know be follow but not care. Too sick care. Think stop, give lymph node for dossier, decide they sick enough already without have something wrong. Drive through San Francisco snow storm, get off Fell Laguna up hill past facelessness, past stores, oh shit forget medical record. Arrive Vet, find twenty foot cage around Vet with hole thirty feet deep dug by big steel Dog with retract claw neck, wheel next feet. New Medicine Sherlock think. Park Toyota last outpost, walk seventeen mile Vet back door, stumble over sixteen amputee War Giraffe, rush look sea, see forty Sea Lion on crutch play badminton. It too much Sherlock think. Go clinic.

Sherlock read paper after House Poodle take Vet Card and sit Sherlock SIT. Read women sex fantasies morning paper, President fuck fantasy social page now page one. Try read Vet's corner, but small Pekinese bark. Sherlock, YOU COME HERE YOU WANT BONE. Sherlock say me want bone, wag ass even though hurt. WHO YOUR NEXT OF DOG? WHO BITCH? Me can't tell. YOU HAVE TELL. WHO NEXT OF DOG? No next of dog. YOU MUST HAVE NEXT OF DOG. No next of dog. Me no tell. No next of dog, no next of dog. YOU MUST HAVE NEXT OF DOG WHO WE CALL LESS YOU DIE.

No know, just fix. Sherlock think retract last statement. Just say me sick dog, no want fix till you fix fixer...get think how all bulldog make all bitch junkie. Give pills, fuck up organ, no pill bulldog, him just humphumphump all time. Too much bullshit Sherlock think as Pekinese point nose down hall GO OUTPATIENT EVALUATION.

Sherlock think pretty interesting all time sign say teach animals how say alphabet. Big pretty interesting all time signs say teach animals alphabet. Big pretty letters say NO SMOKE Area A, AREA B STAND, SHIT, PISS, NOT PISS IN CORNER. Lymph nodes hurt. Sherlock turn corner marked TURN CORNER. Immediate see Afghan Receptionist who say, Who you? Me Sherlock. Got sore prick. Ok, sit down Sore Prick. Alley Cat come take Sherlock blood pressure. Have little claws. Not be in Alley too long. Pump pump pump thump thump thump. Sherlock blood hurry, Sherlock think die. Oh, not now, not now. No temp, little pulse. Ok Sore Prick, have seat. Sore Prick have seat. Hear Afghan talk baby Afghan talk on phone. Hear country club, diaper rash, poddy train, nail polish, sailboat, new dress, crepes. Sherlock look around. This it?

Doe bring coffee to Buck in wheelchair. She smile Doe smile. Smile say, "Hey ole Buck. You wanna come out and play, but can't. Can't do nothin. Come anyway. EAT BARK BUCK!" Double amputee Lion rush into office, wear mod suit, flip stumps, alla time flip stumps, grab paper from Afghan, gone. Sherlock think all whipped animals in wheelchairs. Think about self. Old tired Ram sudden scream, "I don't want my blood pressure taken. You can't have any blood. I gave you all the blood I'm going to give you. Me and my wife paid for a year. We live three hundred and eighty-five dollars a month. I just want results!"

Alley Cat slink. Sherlock think ole tired Ram sound old people in ole Simon and Garfunkel record. Huge Bull lumber in. Have huge beef kidney growing back of ear. Sneer at Sherlock. Toad with respiratory problem lean on cane patiently. Concerned Mrs. Toad look over doctor's shoulder. Read chart belong someone else. Sherlock look up. Ole tired Fish drag fins across floor. Fish have acorn grow out left gill. Sherlock think this not back nature. In come Mr. and Mrs. Hollywood Chicken. Too much Sherlock think.

Hey Sore Prick! Sore Prick stand. Here Sore Prick. Here Sore Prick. Sherlock go room. Hear Mr. Hollywood Chicken say he breathe upside down. How come say Afghan Lady? Door Slam. Sit down Sore Prick. I see you have no next of Dog. No next of Dog. Vet turn radio to 1812 Overture. Sherlock no hear beautiful Siamese walk in say Afghan "Would you hold my beautiful arms?" Afghan say we can't hold your beautiful arms, they're everybody's property, but we can put them on file until doctor comes. Your fur ruffled Sherlock. Sore Prick Vet. Sore Prick. Let's see. Sherlock part fur, pull back. Red mass plop paw. There. See? Have you ever had rabies? No. Tested for? Yes. When? Premarital. Oh. Case history of. . . .Bend over, turn a-round. Uh uh. Have to check for worms. Whoops mit der finger up der ass. Sherlock try claw way up wall, but no get away. That hurt Sherlock? No, it wonderful. Just like rub ass in horseshit. . . Fun fun. Take out stupid. Sherlock too busy hear Siamese say, "Would you hold my beautiful legs?" We can't hold your beautiful legs. They belong to everybody, but we can keep them on file. "Oh thank you Afghan Lady. Here are my beautiful legs." Well Sherlock, it look like you have a virus. I think we'll send you around to Dermatology to see Smokey. Who Smokey? He's skin man. Fur's fine, but the skin. And no rabies. Cough up some blood on the way and we'll test it. Sherlock try. Nothing happen. Vet say try on way.

Sherlock pull fur over prick, step in lobby. See Mr. Hollywood Chicken stand head, breathe in paper bag. New Medicine Sherlock think. Follow yellow brick road cough cough. Go area B, this Area C, sit down, don't smoke fart, breathe, fill necessary forms. Old White Leghorn step on Sherlock paw. Oh, you must be Sore Prick. Sherlock say sometime Sore Prick, sometime Sherlock. Today you're Sore Prick. Right? Riiight? You're to see Smokey. Smokey yes. This is Smokey. Sherlock understand why call Smokey. He talk Smoke. Hi Smokey, me Sore Prick, sometime know as Sherlock. Do come in smoky Smokey.

"Afghan Lady, would you hold my beautiful eyes?" We can't hold your beautiful eyes. "They belong to everyone, but we can put them on file." "Thank you, thank you. Would you mind holding my beautiful mouth too?" "Just on file." Thank you thank you.

You have itititit. Sherlock know itititit. Who your next of Dog? No next of Dog. No next of Dog ok. Bumps on prick not rabies. Virus. HERPES HERPES HERPES. Cure? We have trial method. Huh? "First, you must not humphumphump until bumpy blisters go away. We'll just break blisters. We'll treat it." Nice. "And put this nice red dye on them." Kidding, Sherlock think. "Then put it under fluorescent light for fifteen minutes. You can do it at home for three days." Can't wait. Come on Smokey. You kid. "Sherlock, you just hop up here on the table. This is a scalpel." "NoSHIT! TOO BIG TOO BIG. HURT HURT! OH JESUS...!

"Pull back fur now. That's it. Now hold it. That's it." OH JESUS...CHRIST OH SHIT, THE FUR THE FUR, OH MY DOG, OH MY FUCKING DOG!

Afghan Lady, would you please hold my beautiful body? "Your whole beautiful body?" Yeessssss, oh puulllleeeese? "Well, you know it belongs to everyone?" Oh you can keep it on file. Pleeeease? "I don't know." Oh, thank you wonderful Afghan Lady. Thank you thank you thank you.

Sherlock busy allow scalpel cut neat little prick blisters. Bite foreleg fur. Smokey exhale patient invisible smoke ring. Other room Ole Fish have acorn remove, scales oil. Mr. Toad lean on cane. Burp occasion. Mrs. Toad assist Resident Vet fill chart belong Mrs. Hollywood Chicken who not be treat. Mr. Hollywood Chicken in rest room. Pour air out paper bag. Sherlock definite forget house train. Grit teeth. "There Sherlock, that wasn't so bad now, was it? Here's the dye." No No No, see here, see here. OH OH OH OH JESUS. "Light my dog. Light. The light." Oh thank you Smokey. I am so grateful. "Back in fifteen minutes." Sherlock hold prick under light with paw. "Goooood. That's it. Good dog." Thank you, oh thank you beautiful Smokey. Sherlock begin doze. "TIME'S UP SHERLOCK, TIME'S UP. Now isn't that better?" Oh yes. Oh yes.

Sherlock pull fur down. Smokey give perscription red dye. Sherlock walk slow. Afghan Lady holler, "Hey Sore Prick, turn corner!" Area C, Area B, Area A, NO SMOKE PHARMACY. Name list say PHARMACISTS ADAMS AND AUSTERLITZ. Adams appear window. Look like must be poodle once. Red Dye. "Red Dye?" "Red Dye." "Sit." "Oh, thank you, thank you." "Here go, Red Dye." Oh thank you.

Sherlock walk exit, turn corner. File cabinet in middle hall. Swear. Lift leg, can't, hobble seventeen miles to Toyota. See Mr. Lion referee Giraffes and Sea Lions Badminton. Sherlock smile. Steel Dog stop dig. Sherlock throb. Walk slow. Something drape Toyota steer wheel. Jaqueline Susann tee shirt. Sherlock try. Not right size. Sherlock shrug. Start engine.

Southern Comfort

The fisherman took another hit from the bottle and stared straight across the river where the sun pushed shadows under the brush. As the dirt bike made its way along the shore to his left, a neurotic dog barked several times before being lost in the snap of the bike's engine. Almost thought it would pass on by, but it slowed up, came wide around the fisherman's yellow van and coasted down to the water's edge. He could see the front wheel hesitate in the corner of his right eye, then inch back out of vision.

"Mornin." The engine cut out and a man's voice slipped into the new silence easily. "Whatcha fishin for?"

Now the fisherman turned to the man sitting back on the seat. He watched him push his glasses up on his nose. He watched the sun gleam on his balding head. He looked at the small bike with the blue plastic milk case strapped to the rear fender and he looked at the freshly cut white daisies arranged nicely in a brown clay vase inside the milk case.

"Oh, bass, maybe trout."

"Whatcha usin for bait?"

"Red worms and salmon eggs. Had some clams, but I left em in the refrigerator."

"Oh, you must live around here?"

"Nope." The fisherman looked at the tip of his pole. A horsefly landed on his left wrist and he shook it off. He heard the Southern Comfort slosh in the bottle at his thigh. A full minute passed in blistering silence, then the man turned the key on the right side of the bike. He paused before starting it up.

"Well, I guess anybody can have a refrigerator."

The fisherman kept staring at the tip of the pole and the man rode off until the fisherman could no longer hear the engine. He put the fifth down and reeled in to have a look.

Embarcadero Center

"Want some brandy? Let's sit down."

"This side, can't see the clock from there."

"So who wants to see the clock?"

"I do." He took a hit of brandy and fumbled in his jacket for a cigarette.

"What a beautiful moon and listen to the breeze. It makes the trees sizzle."

"Potted trees. Somewhere between Mahler's Ninth, a four string banjo and a bad case of hemorrhoids. Deodorant and a painting, maybe a harmonica that might sound strange coming from their lips."

"They're not here. I'm here."

"I know you are."

Brenda sat in one of the chairs. The back was wet from an evening hosing. "I wouldn't be here, not if I didn't think you were worth it."

"That's a great snag in the fuselage." He sat down next to her and got right back up. Between the trees, he could see the heavy clock on the Ferry Building hesitate before slipping into nine fifty-six.

Brenda thought about the Great Dane. It had gas. She remembered the vet talking behind the door. A Schnauzer with an older woman sat next to her and kept talking about how tired she was. Sick of serving eggs she said. "Eggs eggs eggs, fried eggs, scrambled eggs, boiled eggs, bacon, poached eggs, ham omelets and homefries. Toast. I hate eggs and omelets and coffee!" She yanked on the dog's chain. The Schnauzer had begun a short bark and came up short. Brenda's tiger cat wailed, its tail thickened, the vet's voice faded to a drone, then rose. "I recommend you shouldn't give Dancer alkaseltzer Theresa. Just keep the diet free of gaseous foods. The Great Dane has a fat stomach and it folds over when he lies down, so that's where the gas gets caught. Of course running helps, but the best. . . ." ". . .and today, this man came in and just as I handed him his eggs, over easy and ham and toast, whole wheat and coffee. . . ." She paused to yank the chain. "He ran his hand up my leg. I mean, I can't stand it. I don't want a man touching me. . . .Touching me and I have to. . . ."

"Here." Richard handed her the brandy. "It is a beautiful city. You can come here with all the dreams and some people should come and ride the cable car and go back home. And the rest. . .well, the guitar player begins with a five dollar axe, a tin cup, a note in the pocket, or possibly on the damn guitar and it becomes more notes. And he goes and visits the dead on certain nights in search of the magic touch. . . .Then an eight hundred dollar job, big thick, great wood and good strings. Just about the time he figures out what the secret is, he's famous, or more than likely not. Then it's booze, blues, whatever and a lot of hangin around. He's forty, tired with a couple of cuts tucked in his case, or kids nobody wants and the blood drips and he hopes the axe'll keep it together. If he's famous, the blood comes in one fell swoop, otherwise drop by drop.

"And the City sits like the Great Nurse by your bedside when you're shitting your brains out. She puts up with your stinking farts, wipes your brow now and then and listens to your obscenities, watches you expose yourself unwittingly and the smiles, the crisp smiles. By the time you figure it out, or find yourself chanting some Indian chant you never heard before, she's home making dinner, trying to stuff somebody else's life in her craw saying you're sick and she was there. And you?

You're eating ice cream and looking at her...and smiling...and you're thankful and you don't even know why."

"I don't think Margaret's like that." Brenda lit a cigarette, inhaled and went on talking with the smoke. "A month ago I called her up and she invited me over for lunch. We sat in the yard. She wore a green halter, white shorts and sandals. The yard was lush with vegetables and I remember how happy she was to see me. Her job was getting her down, but she was there for me and I was too, for her I mean. She gave me some squash from the garden. She seemed so concerned and I was so strung out from the trip. We had lunch and tea. One of the few hot days we have and I was tired. At one point she leaned over and put her hand in mine and asked me if everything was alright and I think she meant it."

"Well, school's out and I'm not up for sitting around the kitchen table with anyone who wants to stuff their spaghetti in my beer glass. There's a cut somewhere that gets lost in the fog and there you are with some strange cock or cunt in your face and don't know how it got there. We're a great breed of dead history flying a 747 all over the sky with a string attached to someone's hand we don't know the name of. The best of us lose crickets, voices and french fries and end up on the block with a piece of lettuce or a potato. A potato, thick and rooted from birth, the dust around its bowels sprouting down there somewhere in the thick night. Not like the tomato that ripens at night; this growls and makes great brown thuds in the earth, as if when it breaks ground, it'll be the thick night itself. Inside its white and wet, it's guts like the bugs on its arms and it walks through the driest desert without so much as a bite. The heavy sound on the inside of us, the filler when the greens run out, but it needs meat and works at the plate for butter and cream. You always dig for it, knowing it's there and it always finds a place at the table when the money's slow. Fried or boiled, baked, creamed or some other absurd presentation, it demands thanks for its nutty little hole in life and we give it as freely as Van Gogh and are astonished at its accomplishments. It piles itself dusty bagged and self important. I might as well have a stone dildo up my ass as talk about it. I stand on the corner and never cease to be amazed at the frenzy and the cyclical frown pulled from the blank windows. And that's where Plain Jane comes walking to the elevator. He doesn't want up, just the hind end of Zen and it walks in swinging asses ahead of him, its light at the top of the stone is only a wet spot on his pants and he knows that's all there really is up there anyway. And knowing it, knowing every curve in the highway doesn't keep him from getting a subtle kick in the middle of the night when he's done everything to keep sane and someone wants the last corner of the blanket."

"I thought about that with Helen. She came over the other night around seven. I'd just finished a salad and a lamb chop. She has a strange smile you know. I can't put my finger on it. Something religious about it; the way it eases itself across her face and hangs patiently, sometimes too much so. *She* told me I looked good. I mean I felt...well, she brought me a small present wrapped in thin maché. A tiny cactus with little furry bristles, not hurting or unpleasant to look at. I offered her some coffee and she told me it was nice to see me again and what was I going to do. I told her I'd been working on a painting. I was painting wings and dolls. I'd done the outline and was playing with colors. I didn't want her to see them yet. She began telling me about the dance she'd choreographed and would I come to see it. She asked me about Mexico and I couldn't talk about it. Too tired and it isn't a three minute subject. Then she went on about some new exercises, meditative, yoga of some kind. She said she'd like to show me sometime. Then she got kind of anxious and came over to the rocker I was sitting in and held out both hands. We went in the bedroom and sat facing each other cross-legged holding hands. We closed our eyes and chanted, then we were silent for a long time. I could smell the perspiration on her neck, but we weren't any closer than this. Suddenly, she just leaned over and put her arms on my shoulders. She looked right through me and started to say something, but caught herself. Finally, she sat back and began telling about a group of women who met every Wednesday. I couldn't click in and I think she felt it. I told her I had to get some sleep and she kissed my cheek and left."

Richard looked at the sky. The clouds moved in an easy hurry catching up with the tops of the buildings and overtaking them. He ran his tongue over the upper left corner of his mouth.

"Most of the time the myth is religion, booze, dope, syphilis or fistfucking, or some other damn thing you can be a card carrying member of, but take a deep breath and someone's there with a paper bag ready to help you learn how to hyperventilate and if you think I'm talking about you, I am. Just try to get on your feet. Try it. The fat'll roll up on your doorstep like a tidal wave. Flags waving, slashing away, throwing question marks through the windows. . .questionnaires. They can't stand it. I know Helen. The gilded face of a past she never had. A book, a kiss and a cactus and a bed full of boredom spilling on the floor . . . .A snail nibbling a leaf after the sun's come up. Hurrying beyond its own hour and not knowing what the hour is. Feelers probing in short little pseudopods designed for wet nights and thank yous. Watch out love. Love me, a canary, a dog, a cat, a snail, love her if she'll let you, but sometimes when a thing is out of its time, it has to go back to the closet to keep the flags off the doorstep. The fat on the doorstep is demanding and degrading, small in an enormous way. Not like the elephant with four knees, no this creature locks itself within itself and can afford to talk about religion, politics and the poor, while the poor are busy being poor and will never be fed. Never, because the fat is based on thank yous and could never live with the idea the poor are eating and not acting the way they teach you to act when you're young. Say thank you to the nice man you poor slob."

"You know there was a guy like that in Mexico. We'd hung our hammocks right near the river. God it was hot. Just before the rainy season. The people camped just a few feet away had just come back from Costa Rica and the driver was trying to fix his bus. His foot was swollen and he told us all of his tools had been stolen in Costa Rica. He'd been walking on a beach and stepped on a ray. It hurt so much he could hardly think and, somehow, he found himself with a woman who said she was a brujo. She made him lie down and then she burned the poison out with a propane torch. It relieved the pain temporarily, but by the time he got to a clinic he had third degree burns and the infection was so bad he couldn't do anything for weeks. I wondered why he didn't find a good doctor. He said something about trying to save money. He seemed like he was in such a good mood. I don't know why he didn't go to a good doctor.

"Don and I were so tired and half strung out that none of it made too much sense anyway, so we went back to the hammocks and flopped, at least for about five minutes. There went the nap with this Mexican family pulling right up to our campsite and turning the car radio on full blast. I thought Don would, well he did almost leap out of the hammock, but I couldn't move. I tried to sleep, then came the beer and everyone running around, so what the hell. More beer and food and finally out came the mescal, not one bottle, but two and I could see it coming. We talked about Mexico and where everyone was from and why Don and I didn't have children. The woman sitting next to me, poked me and when I looked down she was imitating a pair of scissors with her fingers. She pointed at Don with a big question mark in her eyes. God, they must have asked that one eighteen times and down went the mescal. First thing you know it was dark, they were laughing and piling into the car knowing we were just out of our minds. Bang, they were gone and there we were blind and hungry.

"I was so blown out, I couldn't speak *English*, never mind Spanish, but we managed to stumble up to the pavilion that seemed like miles away, maybe it was a hundred yards and the only thing I said was quesadilla and the man said no.

"It was pitch dark except for the sky. Richard the sky began to glow, heat lightning somewhere over the mountains, mosquitos began swarming and high, way up in the trees, somewhere, I'd heard them before at Bonampak, and I guess we were only 150 miles away from it, the chanting began. First the low sound of a sheep baaing, just one, then it sounded like another sheep answered and then, ten maybe twenty, then God it seemed like hundreds. The sky paled and from the hammocks, we could see the tops of the trees sway slightly against the sky a long way up the mountains on the opposite side of the river. It got closer and as it moved across the trees I recognized it. The howler apes moving and the baaaing became more shrill and blended with the breeze. My God there must have been hundreds of them moving across the sky chanting to each other in that long trilling OOOOHOOHOOHOOHOO-HOOOOOOWHOOWHOOWHOOWHOOWHOOO-OOOWHOOOOOOOOO. A symphony, just hundreds and hundreds of apes flowing across the valley just below the sky and the sky flashing yellow heat. It went on for hours and we just looked at the sky and listened. If only I could have written the music. Then I was dozing off. I remember a few toads leaping up and nipping at my butt but I was so tired I couldn't be bothered.

"I was in a mercado, a mercado I had never been in before. It was early morning and along the edge of the stalls was an infinite line of Mayan women sitting in a row. Their noses were perfectly traditional, they wore black skirts and white blouses with embroidery that I couldn't distinguish, and each one had a large clay plate in front of her and on the plate a tall glass which she was spinning between her palms, and in the glass, a fine grained golden maize. The glasses hummed a high pitched crystal sound and I knew this was the final refinement. I looked to my left and another row of Mayan women held blue tin cups. They were dressed exactly the same as the first and they tapped the sides of the cups with short square pieces of wood. Inside the cups the maize was slightly more granular than that in the glasses. The sound of the cups tapped and the whirring of the glasses between the women's fingers was the sound of the apes' symphony across the sky. And I knew, I knew even before I woke up, that somewhere, somehow those apes which can mimic a jaguar or a bird had sung that song. I hadn't been sure at Bonampak. I felt the apes were telling us there was something there, or something had happened there which we could never enter or perhaps shouldn't, but at Palenque when I woke up, I knew. And Richard now I'm back here it seems so frantic."

"Now," he stood up suddenly and spit over the wall, "trees and orgies, apes and cities, don't seem related. A room, a wall, a clock, a bathtub, a strange voice yanking you in the night, a whistle, a steel ball rolling past the painted ladies slapped back several times, but ultimately the long thud, steel on steel in a trough lining wood and perhaps a free game or two, if you match the last number on the board. Very simple, or for Plain Jane walking the city chanting American Zen, getting his pants wet. Best thing he can do under the circumstances. Dammit, where's the brandy?" Brenda reached under the table. She put her hand on his arm and set the bottle on the table. He snatched it up and took a long hot belt, coughed and reached for the cigarettes. "Well let me tell you. Let me tell. I'm gonna," his eyes narrowed, "I'm gonna tell you about Plain Jane. Plain Jane, the one-eyed monster clinging to a moment with the anticipation of a frog on a lily pad, silent to everyone except himself and within, a long croak in a misty night, but no water, the blank face in the mirror, the garden hose sprinkling its own surreptitious harmony, how beautifully decadent you say...Ah." Bending over in the chair, he coughed himself into a short fit, "I'm fine...jusfine...But Jane...Jane is from...yes, you guessed it Bennington...Bennington Vermont...Fred...FRED...just Fred, that's his name...Fred. How do I know? The poor fucker.

"North Bennington...on a farm, with his older brother...who supposedly was retarded, a fat kid with piggy eyes, fat pants and pimples and bigger than the rest of the kids. Used to take Plain Jane and his friends out in the fields in the afternoon and they'd sit around in the cow turds while the brother read from his Snow White coloring book. They had to sit there and never say anything or else he'd slap them, because the thing was, the thing was, he'd be getting off. First thing you know he had it out and be forcing them to pet it while he read the parts about her sleep and the Prince coming and before long he'd be in fits and spasms scaring the kids. Of course he'd pop his cookies all over the book and tell the kids they did it and make them wash the book off. But Plain Jane was interested in other things. Basketball football and not a big kid he tried, his mother working so he could. Father never worked, in fact the farm had a handful of chickens, ducks, one sow, and that was all. Only contribution the father ever made was getting drunk and exposing himself to Fred's friends. 'Whadya think a that? Come in here and take a look at this.' In the meantime, Jane got tied up with hitching to town at night and standing outside the gym watching the kids dance. He'd diddle himself crazy, pick out one he liked and follow her home and look in her window or steal her underwear off the line. By the time he was sixteen he had a bottle swinging in his hand and on a particular night in August he tried to rape or kill some girl, wasn't sure which, but she screamed and he ran. Never caught him but then again they didn't need to. His mother made sure of that. She'd take him in the bathroom, make him take it out and proceed to tell him he ought to keep himself clean, hand him some cotton balls and baby oil. Never made Varsity Basketball. Tried a couple more rapes, unsuccessfully, almost got caught the last time getting stuck in the window with his feet off the ground and all the lights in the house blinking on. Poor little man flailing away to happiness, came home real late and she was waiting. Started marching him to the bathroom. The old man out cold, Fred had a gut full a beer and he waited until she was inside with the door closed and had started her routine, whipped it out and grabbed her by the hair and yanked her right down to the floor and told her to do it. She just lost her mind, oil spilled all over the floor on her hands and his shoes. Began laughing like a madman while she cried, Oh Freddie my Freddie my little Freddie and he just looked down and shook his head and said, Plain Jane you poor wimpy fucker...Oh Plain Jane, Plain Jane, Poor Jane, my God what a mess he was in. But I'm not getting around to it, am I?

"She never did tell the old man, but the older brother got committed. Jane decided he had to get out or be stuck looking at the old man's drunken pecker for the rest of his life, what with all the rapes he hadn't completed, so he joined the Army, managed to get through *it* and then drifted. Somewhere along the line he picked up some skill as a medical technician which he rarely used and I think he, let's see, I met him in Syracuse about the time Wolfert was doing rain dances on South Crouse Avenue and harassing Mr. Blue, who lived in the basement and bought steak for his dog and chewed it up for him because... the dog didn't have any teeth. Jane met this nurse's aide and she was good to him. They fell in love, she had a kid and as poor as they were they tried, but he had Plain Jane locked in and she sensed something, first thing you know...she, was...doing a few...side numbers, I guess, because he caught her in the downstairs apartment and went berserk, found a gun somewhere which turned out to be a blank pistol and dragged her up to his place, brandishing it. Fred, the World War Two tailgunner with the big jumpin eyes stuck his head outta his door on the second floor, popped the eyes real fast and leaped right back in his apartment. When they got upstairs he just dropped her on the bed and stared at her for a long time. Finally threw the gun out the back window, turned around and let the voice drop, 'Plain Jane,' he said, 'Plain fucking Jane.' Now he's here living with someone. She knows about him and doesn't seem to mind, for some reason or another. She's a painter, a good one he says, keeps him fed and all, gives him hot baths in French perfume and bubbles, plays Debussy while he soaks and serves him lemon tea. Don't know what else. . ."

"You know I never could get Don to come with me. He'd rather sit there stoned or swim and when he did come he acted like I was intruding and this was one of his lazy days. Sleeping late and I wanted to go to the ruins so I hitched into town and ate at a little restaurant off the main drag called El Pollo. One of the few places in town where the creeps didn't come and the young boy just out of high school was always nice to me. His mother cooked and he waited tables and did the heavy work. I didn't even tell Don about it because I had to have some place to myself. There were four tables, a crucifix on one wall and the boy's high school diploma on the other. His younger brother brought the juice and changed the records on the old record player just inside the kitchen door. His mother used to come out from time to time and smile. Once she asked me if I was married and rather than disappoint her I said yes, but I couldn't bring myself to say I had children that I didn't have. She was nice about that. So quiet, the chickens clucked in the backyard and the coffee was hot, the eggs OK and I was alone.

"It was still early when I got up there, but hot, oh was it hot, the air was thick with air trying to sleep and the flies floated through it so lazily I thought some of their buzzing must have worn off on it, because I could barely hear them. As if someone had introduced artificial silence into a movie. They do that you know. But it wasn't, it was real, very real and I was alone in this city lying against a jungle. Even the other people who were there didn't seem to be a part of me. All I wanted to do was walk, in fact I climbed the Temple of the Inscriptions and went down to the

Tomb and stayed only a short time. Seemed like a rushed place to be, there at the bottom of that pyramid, very rushed. When I came out I stood for a long time looking down the valley and listening to the silence, but up there the silence was broken every few seconds by a slight breeze or a voice across the way. I heard somebody off to my right, I couldn't tell where exactly, perhaps below on the path, or just above the hill, but it was the only contact and it sounded like someone on the streets here. 'Hey man, this is just like Detroit.' That's what the voice said. 'Just like Detroit.' Can you believe it?

"Then I began to wander between the buildings, sometimes climbing a few steps but not caring so much about that as the experience of the air and the silence. Occasionally I'd run into a Mexican groundskeeper sitting on a rock, but no one really bothered me. At the far end of the ruins, the small stream widens and there's a waterfall and when I found it I took off my sandals and walked into the pool below like it had called me. So damn cool and protected from the sun, the overhanging trees formed an arch around the shallow parts and in the middle where the water was deeper and you could lean against the rocks and let the water cascade over you, the sun was bright and yellow all around. I drenched myself thoroughly and waded to a shallow spot and sat down.

"One of the places where you feel like you're alone at last, and I guess I was for a long time, just sitting there looking at the water against my tummy and wriggling around behind me. Out of nowhere, that's where he must have come from, out of nowhere, this boy waded over to me. I hadn't even seen him. He tapped me on the shoulder and when I turned around his small brown hand was in front of my face. There were several small white stones in it. He said these stones must have been here a thousand years. At first I didn't quite pick up his dialect because he spoke so softly, but when I took the stones and looked them over and saw the tiny fossils of shells implanted in them and looked at the boy's eyes I understood. His eyes were deep with innocence, brown and excited and as we talked they told me he was perhaps fourteen. He hadn't lost the green look boys have, that magic thinness that betrays aggressiveness. He sat down next to me and we played with the stones for a long time, talking about where we were from and how did I like Palenque. He was from Cuernavaca and was with his mother. He said she'd be coming soon and they were going behind the ruins, where they heard there were other ruins. I'd heard that too, but I was skeptical and the water was just so beautiful.

"In a few minutes the mother came to the edge of the water and the boy moved away from me quickly, jumped up and introduced me. She was maybe fifty and wore a broad straw hat, a tan blouse and brown cotton skirt that fell well below her knees. Her face was soft and knowing and not as tan as the boy's body. She smiled and told him to come along if they were going to see the other ruins. One of the groundskeepers, dressed in white pants and shirt barefoot holding his straw hat against his thigh waited on the knoll above her. She asked if I wanted to come too and at first I said no, because the thought of the cool water was more appealing, but the boy, his name was Roberto, convinced me.

"On our way up the hill the mother told me she was widowed. I remember feeling slightly embarrassed as we walked, because the water had soaked every inch of my clothes and I was beginning to sweat again. I kept staring at her dry shoes. She didn't show any signs of perspiration, she talked about our country's closeness and somehow discovered, I spoke better French than Spanish and immediately switched to French, sometimes breaking into English. She thought we had a need for Universality and a common language and said she had a great compassion for the Mexican people trying to adapt to the rapid changes and how it frightened them. She didn't ask me if I was married or why I was alone at Palenque. Roberto walked alternately ahead of us, or behind and the groundskeeper stayed somewhat ahead turning once in a while to make sure we were there. My hair had dried almost completely when we climbed the hill towards the Temple of the Cross. Then I walked ahead with Roberto and the mother walked behind us with the other boy. When we got out of earshot Roberto took my arm lightly and whispered, 'You like Marijuana?' I thought, my God what have I gotten myself in for, but as usual I knew what I'd gotten myself in for. We scrambled on ahead and when I turned around I could see the mother had stopped to rest. Just behind the Temple the path rises sharply and is covered with vines and small trees on either side. Roberto hollered back to say we'd try and find the other ruins. I felt a pit growing somewhere inside of me.

"The climb was more of an expedition. I kept thinking I needed mountain gear, but we hung on to trees and vines, slipping now and then and managed to get up about a hundred yards out of sight before collapsing on a group of vines growing across the path. The path got steeper above and when I turned to Roberto he was busy rummaging through his shirt pocket. We sat there in the soundless heat smoking for what seemed like hours. Once his mother called and he told her we would only go a little farther to see if it leveled off. We were as leveled off as we were going to get. The electricity was deafening, his eyes turned powerful innocence, watered slightly and dried almost immediately. Every part of me screamed no, GOD NO, but I was so innocent myself, so stupidly and beautifully innocent sitting so close to this boy above the whole world. He leaned forward and my insides turned, I thought my heart would leap out and tell him how afraid I was. He seemed so small and his face was so clean and he put his hand to the side of my face, I could barely feel it before he kissed me high on the forehead catching part of my hair on his lips.

"That was all. We began to climb down and it was much more treacherous than coming up. I could see his mother sitting on the ground next to the Temple reading a book and the fear began again. I wasn't sure I could talk to her and when I did make the turn into the light, I slipped and fell scraping my elbow. I wondered what she would say, or if I could even talk, but Roberto was already talking madly and laughing telling her it was too treacherous to climb all the way up. The groundskeeper was gone and his mother helped me up and walked me to the front of the Temple of the Cross which is a very small temple but very special. She stood next to me holding my arm and asked me in English if I had a religion. I knew she was going to have me taken into custody or something, but I blurted out, "Protestant." She smiled and we started down the hill, just she and I. I thought it best to stay away from Roberto for the time being. She wanted to know where I was staying and how long I'd be there. I told her anything. At the bottom of the second hill; there are two hills, one coming down from the Temple of the Cross and another just below the buildings below it, I turned to see where Roberto was. She called him, but he didn't answer and the echo died in the heat ten times thicker than when I arrived and I felt as if I was staring through a clear mist. Then he appeared, to the left of the Tomb, just a hair out of his mother's vision, but I could see him clearly, his head just above the tall grass. He stood for a long time and the air was so thick, so thick, and I knew he was staring at me and I was staring back, but we were beyond staring, the air hissed with the electricity between us, the flies dipped gently and the day burned and burned. He backed into the grass and in a second or two he was running down the hill laughing. I was afraid he was going to fall, but he couldn't, I knew he couldn't. We all laughed and shook hands. Roberto's mother wrote her address on a note pad and gave me the piece of paper and invited me to come stay with them. We all shook hands again and said goodbye. I walked away and didn't dare turn around. On the way out I stopped and bought a bottle of aqua mineral and drank it slowly. A big red and yellow and blue parrot was climbing down one of the poles of the tienda. He was climbing upside down."

"Now I can't follow this like I should, but. . ." Richard stuck his forefinger in some important air next to his right ear, "but it works itself around. I mean, in the City. . .In the City there are lots of chords. Nobody thinks there's really a symphony because they're waiting for a bus or maybe. . . if they did they were reading How to. . .The Perfect Organic Garden. . .or God. . .or how to seduce worms. . .somethin . . .somethin like that, or whatever. . . ."

"And on the train going out there. I mean, Richard, my breasts were sore when we left Mexico City and I couldn't understand why. I thought it might be the pressure change and I said something to Don about it, but he wasn't interested. For some reason, I thought about a girl I'd gone to high school with. She was real thin, but real pretty and brilliant. Little hard on her at first because her father taught English at the school, so everybody kept some distance. Then she met an older boy and thought she was in love with him, but he dumped her. I don't know why, but she turned cold and callous and began screwing like it was just another meal. Something snapped, not the way it came over me when Hap left, but fast. Fast, going so fast. I used to see her father watching her in the halls sometimes and I saw how afraid he was. Then she was gone. Went to Idaho or someplace. Had a scholarship, but she went for the skiing I guess. She was one of the best in the State. I guess things got a lot faster because just before I left for New York, I heard she got killed in a car crash coming back from a skiing weekend. I thought about Hap and it made me shudder. There I was on a train ten years later thinking about her lying dead in the snow somewhere. Why? My breasts were sore and I knew I wasn't pregnant.

"In the middle of the night, I woke up and blew my nose. The click of the wheels was slow and I knew we were going downhill. Then I was blowing my nose every five minutes trying hard not to wake Don and not wanting to climb down to the bathroom. In the morning the pillow was covered with blood. Don passed it off as an altitude change. I wasn't hungry, so I waited until they folded the beds up and sat for hours looking out the window at the fields and somewhere a long way off, I knew there were trucks, hundreds of trucks and red dust. I thought about red dust and skin and dried blood. And the children, millions of children running to Mexico City smiling, not running, but driven and never able to turn back.

"And we were going to Yucatan on this train. The day before we'd been to the museum and I still heard the conch echoing every half hour or so. It sent chills up my spine and the train clicking clicking underneath us. Going to Yucatan. The train going very slow and so much to think about. Levels of the pyramids began as levels to keep the rain out of the houses becoming bigger and bigger until they almost touched the rain again and that wasn't enough, the signs on the remotest buildings ORANGE CRUSH ORANGE CRUSH COCA COLA MODELO MODELO the train backing up, another train passing in the opposite direction, a soldier in that train. I could see his silhouette. He took off his pack and slung it on the overhead rack and put his rifle next to the seat. For a second I thought I'd see his face as he leaned towards the window, but our train lurched and he was gone.

"Later in the club car I drank beer with Don and talked with some other people from Toronto. I wasn't really listening. Somewhere in the car a man talked about his job with the American Legion in San Salvador and across the way an older Mexican couple sang Frank Sinatra songs to each other in Spanish. One of the songs the one they sang over and over again was Strangers In The Night.

They were having such a good time. The table in front of me had a bridge game going that went on and on. Probably wouldn't have payed any attention except one of the women was sick and kept upchucking in napkins. Once she missed and splattered her partner's shoes, but she wouldn't leave the table. Her husband begged her to go back to the compartment but she told him in very good English to go fuck himself. Someone said, 'I haven't heard Yiddish in years.'

"We crossed the Rio Coatzocualcos as the sun went down. It was flat and calm with many tributaries and a strong smell of chemicals. I was beginning to see lots of turkeys. By morning everyone was half crazy; Irvine with his honesty and valium, Cindy with her liberation and bitchiness and the puking. McGuiness with his slow Spanish and pipe, his dying withered up wife, Don just as drunk as he could be and the Mexican lovers kept on loving each other. I was so excited I couldn't think about all the things I wanted to do. We were going to the old cities. The thought of a train going back in there was frightening. Richard, did you know Crispin never got to Yucatan? Isn't that something? My breasts weren't sore anymore."

A careen of headlights followed the building around the corner three blocks away and leaped into Richard's eyes as they bounced up and over the trolley tracks. He sat down quickly and covered his face with his hands. "Don't let 'em see me, just don't, please don't let 'em see me."

"What is it? What is it?" She knelt in front of him and tried to pry his hands away. "Who are they?"

When he heard the car pass beneath him he dropped his hands. "Forget it, Brenda, just forget it."

"How can I forget it? It's like me asking you to forget your friends or Hap. I don't even know what it's about. Ok Richard, Ok." She sat back down. "How did you know about Jane?"

"He told me. But the tail end of the thing is. . .is. . .the brother. . .they found out he wasn't retarded. . .just repressed and he got outta that place. . .got married went to some little school in the Midwest and began writing poetry. Even got a teaching job, but he couldn't hold it. Flipped his wig and had to move on. Jane told me he's on a funny farm up north a here writing Haiku and God knows what all else. He. . Jane that is, goes up every few months and brings him books. Last Jane told me he had a coffin built in his room with a mannequin of Snow White in it and was writing reviews for some half-assed little newsletter. . .in the Midwest. . .Jane mails them sometimes. He's famous. They like his reviews. Jane keeps telling me he's going to bring me some. . .reviews but. . .you know how that goes. . . ."

He tried to get up and fell back in the chair, tried again. He staggered slightly, bumping Brenda's knee and shuffled across the overpass and looked at the clock. "What does all this have to do with anything? Anything Brenda."

"Yeah," she said. "What does this have to do with Helen or Margaret?"

"Helen or Margaret. Reentry into the atmosphere, burning up at both ends, tail spins and sauerkraut, turkeys and apes, trains and brandy, hot dogs and. . . ."

"Helen, Richard, Helen."

"Ah yes, Helen. And Hector, you remember Hector doncha' Brenda?"

"You're not going to use that on me are you?"

"What's wrong with Hector?"

"Nothing's wrong with Hector. You're drunk."

"Is this where we've come from? Is this what we've come to? A trail of alligators crawling down the avenues in slow motion, the *Something* we need to keep around in case, in case we MIGHT, just might want to hear it? Give it a-way. Throw it away. I say throw the whole fucking thing in the drink. Bye bye so long. Throw the GOD DAMN rag over the side."

"I can't throw everything away. Not everything. Some of those people are dear to me. I grew up with them. Like Doreen."

"Doreen the skiing casualty. Humph. I appreciate that, but it doesn't have to control. . . ."

"It doesn't control Richard."

"It does control, don't you get it? Murder in the City. Silent cold-blooded murder. Not even calculated. . .or calculated. . . whichever comes first."

"Where do I fit in Richard? I'm there alright, but there's something else. I have the greatest urge to say. Hello how are you, a robot Hello. HOW. . .ARE. . .YOU? WHAT. . .DO. . .YOU. . .HAVE . . .TO. . .TELL ME? YES. I. . .AM. . .TALKING. . .TO. . .YOU. . .OH THAT. I HEARD THAT BEFORE. WHAT ELSE DO YOU HAVE TO SAY? I HEARD THAT ONE TOO. WELL ANYTHING ELSE? OH. I HAVE NOTHING TO CONTRIBUTE. I GO NOW." Brenda wandered aimlessly and stiff legged bumping into tables and the wall. "HI. . .HOW. . .ARE. . .YOU. . ? WHAT DO YOU HAVE TO SAY FOR. . .YOURSELF. . .TODAY. . ? I. . . HEARD. . .THAT. . .ONE. . .BEFORE. . .BEFORE. . .BEFORE. . . ANYTHING. . .ELSE. ? .ELSE. ? .ANYTHING. . .ELSE. ? .I HEARD . . .THAT. . .WHAT ELSE. ? .WHATELSEWHATELSEWHATELSE?

MUST GO NOW....MUST GO NOW...." She bumped into a table, slid around the edge and fell haphazardly in the chair. "I GO NOW. See Richard, there doesn't seem to be a place for a straight answer. Where in the hell are they? False intimacy kills me. It makes knots inside, twisted light-headed knots that don't go away and I'm spinning around and around........FUCK!"

He stood on the chair and leaned on the wall. He unbuckled his pants, slid them down with his undershorts and leaned on the concrete again. "Refreshing as an ice cream cone. The past fallen down and kicking. One minute it tells you how to plant a garden, and the next, the vegetables are rotting on the kitchen table. You're worrying about freezing your ass off and the next minute you remember sitting on the outhouse boards in the middle of the Winter wasn't that bad, but we go right on freezing our ass off because it's convenient and almost more pleasant than steaming shit in its midst. And the latter." He spread his cheeks and sat again, "The latter, the most beautiful soup to swim in, providing you know what soup is. A dream stopped in the middle cries help, a lonely cat on a backyard fence can turn its yellow eyes from the light, curls the tail around its rump and waits, while we pace impatiently up and down history looking for a new gun. Nine times eight is seventy-two and the cat isn't thinking much about multiplication tables. God this feels good. Another tear in last year's milkshake'll set off a catastrophe, while the cat sits and waits never knowing when time begins or ends. We're dated the second we're born and the past pulls the feathers off the chickens without any knowledge of hot water or fingers, it knows the pores tighten with a pull and slacken immediately and when they dilate, it just eases us naked without so much as an apology or a contract. And we believe it's cunning and sleep in its bed, short sheeted and moaning. We know how cold it is, and breathe in its indignations and a sorry bunch we are, shoveling snow like madmen, heart attacks and blisters. The second the temperature drops we're beside ourselves shoveling, and the snow keeps coming down."

"Kick it out Richard, why don't we just kick it outta our lives and be done with it? I can't keep this up the rest of my life. I could buy a pencil and erase the tracks for hours. Jesus!"

"Well you got no corner on that sweetheart."

"Walk away then."

"A cat with a brain and no tail falls a long way."

"Or television with the image too large for the screen. Someone gets strangled and you never see the act, just a throttle and a slump, a commercial within a commercial. Chicken bones and jesus. Richard, I want somebody there. Is there something wrong with that? I don't want their blood.

"I know you don't." He zipped his pants. "I know you don't and neither do I. I love you Brenda and what the hell good does it do?"

"Come on, forget the dramatics."

"Oh, too good for dramatics? What have we been talking about?"

"The price of popcorn."

"I'm thinking we've been talking about that." He slid into the chair and lit a cigarette. "No, not that simple. I wake up in the middle of the night, my heart's thumping, a dog down the block is yelping, or the little man with the long black coat and the pipe stump with the cigar sticking out of it is baying underneath my window. You remember him. He stands under the overpass at the East Bay Terminal and talks to himself. Remember one morning we walked by and he waited until we passed and yelled, 'Oh Yeaaaaahhh?'"

"Oh I remember him alright."

"Oh come on Brenda. He thought you were nice and, well, how's an ole guy like that gonna." He laughed to himself. "There's no answer. Which one would you believe? Don't tell me. But, I wake up in yesterday and it's still snowing. Maybe I can't let the snow stop. Get to kickin around and well, maybe, it might be the hardest winter of all. Standing, shifting weight from heel to toe in the damn cold. Waiting for god knows what. For him, there's an afternoon, a morning, a steel night and still, that guy has a route he travels every day. Don't think he wants to ride the merry-go-round, but...we feed too many wooden horses anyway. Brenda, what makes us so washed and at the same time drunk with ourselves?"

"Richard, if I could only let you give me what you say and not want more. It's breaking me. I could believe Bogart who said people who talk about sex, but he didn't have to. Jesus shit, so a woman lives in somebody else's myth for ten or fifteen years and lands a little corner of the world on somebody else's fingerprints. What the hell good is that when you're fifty or sixty? I can take the smell of your farts, but remember, I get sick too and rotting away from the waist down isn't something I read in the funny papers. Little Orphan Annie I ain't, and won't be, and I hate that from Helen or Margaret more than I could ever think about with you. Wearing a dress might be a dream, but sometimes for me it's real bright and I like to sing thinking about it and I like your song when you decide to sing it, which isn't often enough, but I don't like waiting for you to decide. And I'm not running away from what's not between my legs to please you or anybody else. I'm too good with my fingers and their tongues down there haven't convinced me yet, although I'll tell you Richard, it certainly isn't the beginning or the end of the world for either of us. Is it?"

Richard couldn't get his bearings, the chair was uncomfortable and the brandy suddenly too bitter, so he made his way to the wall and held his breath for a few seconds, then took some good deep ones. "I feel like I'm catching a bus for the wrong side of town and can't tell the driver to tell me where the transfer point is, never mind get him to give me a transfer. What am I?"

"For chrissakes, you're an asshole. What else did you have on your mind?"

"Well, having a cock in your mouth and a popper in your nose under the eucalyptus trees with the expectation of having to run can be easier and a lot more satisfying sometimes, but bruised ankles and running into fences with a headlight behind you makes you wonder. A baby's born feet or head first, then comes the rest. We carry that like a whore on Saturday night, or a dead fool waiting. The hiss of trees and branches scraping the window is what might have been kneeling or triumphant. Ten years walking, six months dancing and a lot of ground to cover. . . ."

"Richard. . .Richard. I want more. Is that so wrong?"

"Depends on what more means."

"Look. Ten years walking. So what? Walking through, yes, but walking. Uhuh. I can dance and I'm damn sure going to, but making room to dance can be six into ten which is one plus and that's alright isn't it? I mean it could be thirty crawling, thirty falling."

"Listen. How about Joe Gilmore the war hero? You know him. Everybody knows him. It's all pure theater. . .all theater." He broke into a demonic laugh. "That's all. . .theater. Put a hero on stage. Step right up ladies and gentlemen. . .and now we come to the stuurangest phenomemmemum ever witnessed. . .

ever witnessed," he burped, "By man woman or beast. You see...Now the way to keep from lying is, is of course to wear a uniform and smoke a cigar...Facts of life...Didja ever meet a cigar smoker that lies? I mean a real down to earth Havana sucker may bullshit but..." He raised his forefinger. "But, he never lies. Get yourself a fat corona, shove it in your mug and you are gonna be the best-most-honest-heel-clickin-wallawalla, step right up see the incredible man and his dog...From the far corners of...the earth...we bring you this friendly and harmless extravaGANZA...ZZAA. Notice the woolywooly fur and the Pendleton church, I mean shirt. Only at this time, now ladies and gentlemen, I assure you this couple is authentic. This man, will for the sake of the disbeliever...for a mere one dollar extra... take off his shirt and the fur of his dog will be parted, so you see we have gone to the utmost and expended valuable time and fundzzzz, fundzzzz, to present to you on this night of nights the INCREDible MANIFESStation of.... Yes, we have Optimo Admirals and for those faint of heart...pipes with Borkum Riff whiskey." He paused and pointed to one of the crowd. "Briar? How about a corncob? I see young lady, you are a skeptic. Well, the world is known for that and we certainly can't blame an intelligent woman as yourself for doubting the authenticity of...I see you are about to infer that I am getting...wet...that you doubt my motives...that you think all this...is all and there you sit in your splendor while I...I DUCK...I duck swim HOOOOWAACK, WAKWAKWAK-WAKWAKWAK! Go ahead and laugh. Go ahead...Lookit this duck neck. Hoooooowack. You will see this as a moment of...them...but...but this duck is not housebroken. They say you can housebreak a duck. I repeat, not housebroken... Notice the wings." The water soaked his belly from crotch to chest. "The wings. Do come here dear skeptic. Come lie with me in the, come swim with me in the great pond HOOOOO-WACK!" He began doing spins on his belly. Brenda got in the water and began swimming. "Hooowack hoowack wack wack wack wack." Brenda flapped her wings. "Hoowack wack wack. WAKWAKWAKWAKWAK." Then they were swimming silently across the azure pool, the lily pads touched their feathers lightly, little frogs croaked as they followed the undertow, then alternated following each other, drifting in and out around the wonderful pool and the rushing swirl and the rushing swirl. When they reached the small sandbar, they paused to look at each other, touching faces and wet shaded breath and somewhere on the other side, a nightwatchman rubbed his chin and shook his head before calling in.

"I think I heard a duck."

"A what?"

BIOGRAPHY

David Plumb lives with the poet Julia Vose. He has been an ambulance driver, a hot dog vendor, janitor, yogurt packer, farm hand, movie projectionist, lab technician, slaughterhouse worker, cook, Gunnery Officer in Vietnam and the author of four books. He holds a degree in political science from Syracuse University and presently resides in Northern California with two cats, Pablo, Candice and the rest of the chickens.

Titles by Wings Press

Robert Bonazzi *Fictive Music*
Susan Bright *julia*
Judson Crews *Nolo Contendere*
Eleanor Earle Crockett *Two Poems*
David Gene Fowler *Brief Case*
M.W. McGee *Ambrosia Dancing at Mary's*
Vassar Miller *Approaching Nada*
Vassar Miller *Small Change*
David Plumb *The Music Stopped and
   Your Monkey's on Fire*
Townes Van Zandt *For the Sake of the Song*
Michael Ventura *The Mollyhawk Poems*
A.D. Winans *Venus in Pisces*

P.O. Box 25296
Houston, Texas 77005
713-668-7953

```
R0142652186    TXR    T
                      813
       7.50           P734


PLUMB, DAVID
       MUSIC STOPPED AND
YOUR MONKEYS ON FIRE
```

DISCARD